Gabrielle Roy

Twayne's World Authors Series

French Literature

David O'Connell, Editor
University of Illinois

TWAS 726

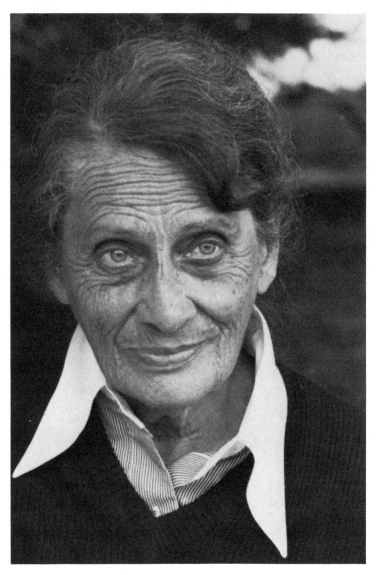

GABRIELLE ROY
(1909–1983)
Photograph courtesy of Alain Stanké

Gabrielle Roy

By M. G. Hesse
University of Lethbridge

Twayne Publishers • Boston

Gabrielle Roy

M. G. Hesse

Copyright © 1984 by G. K. Hall & Company
All Rights Reserved
Published by Twayne Publishers
A Division of G. K. Hall & Company
70 Lincoln Street
Boston, Massachusetts 02111

Book Production by Marne B. Sultz
Book Design by Barbara Anderson

Printed on permanent/durable acid-free
paper and bound in the United States of
America.

Library of Congress Cataloging in Publication Data

Hesse, M. G. (Marta Gudrun)
   Gabrielle Roy.

   (Twayne's world authors series; TWAS 726)
   Bibliography: p. 107
   Includes index.
   1.   Roy, Gabrielle, 1909–   —Criticism and
interpretation. I. Title.   II. Series.
PQ3919.R74Z659   1984   843   83-22663
ISBN 0-8057-6573-5

Contents

About the Author

M. G. Hesse is Professor and Chairman of the Department of Modern Languages at the University of Lethbridge, Lethbridge, Alberta, Canada. She graduated from the University of Toronto with a Ph.D. in French where she was a recipient of Province of Ontario Graduate Fellowships.

She has held research grants from the University of Lethbridge and the Social Sciences and Humanities Research Council of Canada. Her publications include *Porte Ouverte* (Book Society of Canada, 1974), *Approaches to Teaching Foreign Languages* (North-Holland, 1975), *Women in Canadian Literature* (Borealis, 1977), *Hermann Hesse and Romain Rolland* (Humanities, 1978), *Childhood and Youth in Canadian Literature* (Macmillan, 1979). Her work has appeared, among other places, in *Mosaic, L'Action Nationale, Journal of Canadian Fiction, The Canadian Fiction Magazine, Western Humanities Review, New Orleans Review, the Malahat Review, Confrontations,* and the *Journal of Popular Culture.*

Preface

Until now, no comprehensive study in English has been published to give a general account of Gabrielle Roy's achievements. This is somewhat surprising for a writer of her stature (although her work has been discussed in numerous reviews, articles, and theses). The focus of this introductory study is therefore a critical analysis of Gabrielle Roy's works with varying emphasis on the plot, characterization, and themes determined by the particular character of each book. Also, in light of Gabrielle Roy's art, a discussion of the structure and style in a narrow sense would seem more appropriate for another more specialized study.

The outstanding success of *Bonheur d'occasion (The Tin Flute)* assured Gabrielle Roy almost immediately an international reputation on a scale unprecedented for any other Canadian writer. The honors bestowed on the author of this first novel included the prestigious Prix Fémina in 1947 in France and for its English version, *The Tin Flute,* the Governor General's Award in Canada. The book was also chosen as a Literary Guild selection in the United States.

Gabrielle Roy is without question one of Canada's most respected and widely read writers. But while her books are well known, she personally remains a relatively unknown figure. Early in her career she decided that she had to withdraw from the limelight to allow her creative impulse full development and to let her books speak to her.

Much of Gabrielle Roy's work, however, is of a very personal nature: particularly the semiautobiographical sketches of *Rue Deschambault (Street of Riches)* and *La Route d'Altamont (The Road Past Altamont),* as well as *La Montagne secrète (The Hidden Mountain)* which embodies much of her philosophy of art. This study therefore begins with a biographical sketch intended to familiarize the reader with the author's background and to limn the sources of her inspiration that are profoundly linked to her Canadian experience. The consciousness and vitality of her French heritage account for Roy's decision to establish her residence in Quebec and to write in French.

A strict chronological order has not been observed so as to allow us to focus on the essential unity of the work of the author who has always been striving to bring to her readers, as she terms it, "more knowledge, more sympathy, more love."[1]

In "The Urban Novels", chapter 2, we deal with *Bonheur d'occasion* and *Alexandre Chenevert (The Cashier)*. In the former work the novelist presents with uncompromising realism a social fresco of the poor in the metropolis of Montreal during the Depression and at the beginning of World War II. Gabrielle Roy at once narrows and expands her vision in *Alexandre Chenevert*. As the humble bank teller questions the meaning of life and probes the mystery of suffering, the reader soon recognizes in the protagonist both Everyman and an exceptional individual. The stylistic excellence of these two early novels illustrates par excellence Gabrielle Roy's power of empathy and her artistic skill in communicating this to her readers.

Idyllic Interludes, chapter 3, introduces the first of the author's Manitoban works, *La Petite Poule d'Eau (Where Nests the Water Hen)*. This charming title recalls the small island in northern Manitoba where Roy spent one summer as a schoolteacher. Drawing on her experiences in the 1930s, the author re-creates for her readers in a spirit of rare humor the idyllic existence of the Tousignants. The feeling of nostalgia underlying this work is that however utopian the life she portrayed may appear, it was or could be within our reach. This sentiment is even more pronounced in *Cet été qui chantait (Enchanted Summer)*. But here the animal and plant world becomes the principal actor, and man's role is essentially that of an observer.

Rue Deschambault and *La Route d'Altamont,* the focus of attention in chapter 4, represent for many of Gabrielle Roy's readers her most admired works. In both volumes the author in the guise of Christine takes her readers on a pilgrimage to the past. As she "transfigures" the experiences of her childhood and youth, Gabrielle Roy introduces her delighted readers to the daily happenings and characters of her "Street of Riches," where the sensitive child discovers a world of love and security, joy and sorrow, truth and hypocrisy. The importance of childhood, the relation between the young and the old, and the sources of Christine's artistic aspirations are of major interest in these sketches.

The artist's vocation comes to the forefront in *La Montagne secrète,* as suggested in the title of chapter 5, "An Artist's Credo." Gabrielle Roy's choice of a painter as her model and pseudospokesman gave her at once greater freedom and presented a challenge. As a novel it is perhaps the least successful of her works. Yet *La Montagne secrète* is essential for a better appreciation of the creative process as Roy understands it, particularly with regard to the act of self-discovery, the search for perfection, and the artist's role in society vis-à-vis his fellowmen.

"Worlds in Conflict," chapter 6, marks to some extent a return to the world of *Bonheur d'occasion.* The Eskimo's conflict between his traditions and the white man's way of life arouses the indignation of the author of *La Rivière sans repos (Windflower).* Here the novelist's exceptional empathy is illustrated in the forceful portrayal of an Eskimo mother. The loss of her son, born of a white father, epitomizes the tragic existence of these northern people. The indictment of the white man's values is particularly effective because the author refrains from didacticism.

Un jardin au bout du monde (Garden in the Wind) and *Ces enfants de ma vie (Children of My Heart)* are discussed in chapter 7, "The Canadian Mosaic." In these collections of short stories Gabrielle Roy draws again on her experiences in Manitoba. Her French-Canadian heritage and her father's occupation as an immigration officer have made her especially conscious of Canada's multinational identity. This awareness has found lasting expression that is unique in Canadian literature with regard to both its depth and breadth. Gabrielle Roy feels compelled to heed these people's unspoken command to "tell their story" so that she may give them existence. As she traces the lives of these individuals isolated by personal and social, or cultural and linguistic barriers, the author is motivated by the belief in the brotherhood of all men.

This study concludes with a general estimate of Gabrielle Roy's achievements. She deserves a truly international reading public because her work is on the one hand representative of the best in Canadian literature, and on the other hand these writings that are so deeply rooted in the author's Canadian experience give expression to universal values.

I have benefited during the preparation of this work from the support of the University of Lethbridge and the Social Sciences and Humanities Research Council of Canada. I should also like to express sincere thanks to my editor, Dr. David O'Connell, for his support and cooperation.

M. G. Hesse

University of Lethbridge

Acknowledgments

For permission to reprint copyright material, grateful acknowledgment is made to the following authors and publishers:

Madame Gabrielle Roy for permission to quote excerpts from *Alexandre Chenevert, Bonheur d'occasion, Ces enfants de ma vie, Cet été qui chantait, Fragiles lumières de la terre, Un jardin au bout du monde, La Montagne secrète, La Petite Poule d'Eau, La Rivière sans repos, La Route d'Altamont, Rue Deschambault.*

From *The Cashier, The Tin Flute, Children of My Heart, Enchanted Summer, The Fragile Lights of Earth, Garden in the Wind, The Hidden Mountain, Where Nests the Water Hen, Windflower, The Road Past Altamont,* and *Street of Riches* by Gabrielle Roy reprinted by permission of the Canadian publishers McClelland and Stewart, Limited, Toronto.

Donald Silver Cameron for permission to quote excerpts from *Conversations with Canadian Novelists.* Alain Stanké for kind permission to use the Gabrielle Roy frontispiece photograph.

Chronology

1909	Gabrielle Roy born 22 March in Saint-Boniface, Manitoba, Canada, the youngest daughter of Léon Roy, a government immigration officer, and of Mélina Landry.
1915–1927	Studies at the Académie Saint-Joseph in Saint-Boniface.
1927	Death of Gabrielle Roy's father.
1927–1929	Teacher training at the Winnipeg Normal Institute.
1929–1937	Teaches in several schools, including La Petite Poule d'Eau.
1937–1939	Begins sojourn in Europe. Publishes her first newspaper articles.
1939	Returns to Canada and decides to live in Montreal. Pursues career as a journalist.
1943	Death of Gabrielle Roy's mother.
1945	*Bonheur d'occasion (The Tin Flute)*.
1946	Médaille Richelieu from the Académie canadienne-française.
1947	Prix Fémina and Lorne Pierce Medal of the Royal Society of Canada for *Bonheur d'occasion*. Governor General's Award for *The Tin Flute*, the English version of *Bonheur d'occasion*. *The Tin Flute* is a monthly selection of the Literary Guild of America. Is elected to the Royal Society of Canada, the first woman to be so honored. Marries Dr. Marcel Carbotte.
1947–1950	Sojourn in France.
1950	*La Petite Poule d'Eau (Where Nests the Water Hen)*.
1950–1952	Returns to Canada and lives in Montreal.
1952	Establishes permanent residence in Quebec City.
1954	*Alexandre Chenevert (The Cashier)*.
1955	*Rue Deschambault (Street of Riches)*.
1956	Prix Duvernay of the Saint-Jean Baptiste Society of Quebec for her work.

1957   Governor General's Award for *Street of Riches*, the English version of *Rue Deschambault*.

1961   *La Montagne secrète (The Hidden Mountain)*.

1966   *La Route d'Altamont (The Road Past Altamont)*.

1967   Companion of the Order of Canada.

1968   Canada Council Medal for her work.

1970   *La Rivière sans repos (Windflower)*.

1971   Prix David award from the Quebec Government for her work.

1972   *Cet été qui chantait (Enchanted Summer)*.

1975   *Un jardin au bout du monde (Garden in the Wind)*.

1976   *Ma Vache Bossie*, a children's story.

1977   *Ces enfants de ma vie (Children of My Heart)*.

1978   Governor General's Award for *Ces enfants de ma vie. Fragiles lumières de la terre, (The Fragile Lights of Earth)*, a collection of miscellaneous writings originally published between 1942 and 1970.

1979   *Courte-Queue (Cliptail)*, a children's story, is published.

1980   Canada Council's Prize for Children's Literature for *Courte-Queue*.

1982   *De quoi t'ennuies-tu, Eveline?*

1983   Gabrielle Roy dies 13 July in Quebec City.

Chapter One
The Development of a Writer

An Auspicious Beginning

In *Rue Deschambault* (*Street of Riches*, 1955) Christine, the central character who frequently serves as a fictional spokesman for Gabrielle Roy, is intent on defining her aspirations as she contemplates the choice of a career. "And the happiness the books had given me I wished to repay. I had been the child who reads hidden from everyone, and now I wanted myself to be this beloved book, these living pages held in the hands of some nameless being, woman, child, companion, whom I would keep for myself a few hours."[1] It is fortunate for Gabrielle Roy's readers that Christine's dream has been amply realized by her creator.

Gabrielle Roy's first novel *Bonheur d'occasion* (*The Tin Flute*, 1945) was awarded the Prix Fémina in 1947. For the first time since its inception in 1904 the jury honored a foreign writer in giving this prestigious prize to a French-Canadian author. In 1946 she had been awarded the Médaille de l'Académie canadienne-française. In the United States *The Tin Flute* became a Literary Guild selection. Thus Gabrielle Roy was assured almost immediately a large international audience. This public recognition of a first novel rewarded an author whose "apprenticeship" had been served as a journalist in France and in Canada. It gave her the impetus and conviction to pursue her career as a writer.

But who is Gabrielle Roy, readers and critics began to ask themselves. To a large extent their curiosity would not be satisfied, then or in later years. Having interviewed Roy in 1950, fellow-novelist Ringuet,[2] concluded he did not know anyone "more secretive."[3] Her natural reluctance to reveal herself and her private life to the public is strengthened by her concept of art. "The duty of a writer is to write. His books speak for him."[4] Nevertheless, Gabrielle Roy's occasional French or English interviews and miscellaneous "memories" over the past thirty-five years do provide important insights into the interrelation between the author's life and her creative process. As Roy recalls persons and events of her childhood and early adulthood, she identifies the most noteworthy sources of her creative writings, and we realize how successfully she blends "Poetry and Truth" (as Goethe termed his autobiography)—particularly in her two semi-autobiographical collections of vignettes and short stories, *Rue Deschambault* (*Street of Riches,* 1955) and *La Route d'Altamont* (*The Road Past Altamont,* 1966).

Inasmuch as Roy remains deeply attached to her prairie background and finds the inspiration of a major part of her work in her childhood, it behooves us to examine her background more closely.

Background

Gabrielle Roy was born in 1909 in Saint-Boniface, Manitoba. In this French-speaking enclave in Canada's predominantly English-speaking West she grew up with strong family ties and traditions, a profound respect and love for her French and Quebec heritage, as well as an intense awareness and appreciation of language.

Roy's identification with the past of her ancestors was to be given artistic expression in *Rue Deschambault* and *La Route d'Altamont,* and undoubtedly explains also her great empathy for Canada's many immigrants whose yearning for the future is intimately linked to preserving the roots of the past, as seen, for example, in her collection of short stories *Un jardin au bout du monde* (*Garden in the Wind,* 1975).

Gabrielle Roy's maternal grandparents had come to Manitoba from Quebec. Nostalgia for the Laurentian Mountains of their native province determined the choice of their new home. But Grandfather's expectations were disappointed. The Pembina Hills could not assuage his wife's homesickness. The ambivalent love for both the mountains and the plains is a family trait that Roy traces to her grandfather. This quality has a special significance for her as an artist because this "divided love . . . [is] also an inexhaustible source of dreams, of confidences, of leavings and 'travellations' such as few people knew to the extent we did, a family that was horizon-bound, if there ever was one. And of course it is in their divided love that artists and others find their hurts and treasures."[5] And this love for both the prairie and mountains, as will be noted in our discussions of *Rue Deschambault* and *La Route d'Altamont,* becomes the source of several nostalgic and humorous anecdotes.

Although Gabrielle Roy never knew her grandfather personally, he became a living presence for her. The family's remembrances of this pioneer fascinated the future writer who observed that everyone "painted him in his own image."[6] Such personal interpretation or embellishment is a vital aspect of Gabrielle Roy's art. The idea that "the artist adds a little of himself to his creation"[7]—as Roy notes as she contemplates her portrait by the Quebec artist Jean-Paul Lemieux— occasionally assumes such importance in her own writing that the distinction between reality and imagination may become obliterated. Thus the author refers to Sam Lee Wong, one of the principal characters in *Un jardin au bout du monde (Garden in the Wind),* as "doubtless the most solitary creature of creatures I ever met or invented."[8]

The contrast between the grandparents seemed so striking that Roy's memories of her grandmother evoke a sense of strength, visually linked with the image of the prairie's great grain elevators. "Ma grand-mère toute-puissante" ("My Almighty Grandmother"), the first selection of *La Route d'Altamont,* is a loving, semifictionalized tribute to that proud woman.

Gabrielle's parents, Léon and Mélina Roy, were also two very different natures. Elements of their characters served, as will be seen later, also in *Rue Deschambault,* notably in the selection with the revealing title "Le Jour et la nuit" ("By Day and by Night"). The mother's unfailing cheerfulness contrasted with the older man's melancholy that was apparently rooted in the hardships of his youth.

This "self-made" man of pioneering stock became a highly respected colonization agent for the federal government among the Ruthenians, Dukhobors, Mennonites, and Hutterites whose settlement he supervised, principally in Saskatchewan. Léon Roy's own background largely explains his great understanding and empathy for the settlers of so many nations, but he was forced into an early retirement in 1913 because he refused to change his political allegiance when the Progressive Conservatives assumed power under the leadership of Robert Borden in 1911. Thus Léon Roy made a sacrifice that went beyond economic hardships for his family. Roy's most poignant memories of her father—a disillusioned man, broken in spirit and in health, when his youngest daughter knew him—are vividly re-created in "Petite Misère" in *Rue Deschambault.*

Gabrielle Roy recognizes in herself not only her father's tendency toward sorrow but also her mother's joyous nature. With delight the author recalls her mother's adventurous spirit and that unforgettable journey to her new home when Mélina was just a little girl.

Mélina Roy's numerous stories surrounding that unforgettable adventure of her childhood transmitted to her youngest child the enchantment of that trip across the unknown land that seemed like a sea voyage on an uncharted ocean. And, as readers of *Rue Deschambault* and *La Route d'Altamont* can readily testify, Gabrielle Roy has never outgrown that enchantment of her childhood. She accepts both her mother's need for "embellishment" and her father's concern with such lack of truthfulness. "Both were right."[9]

This ability to reconcile differences was to become a major source of inspiration for Gabrielle Roy.

The Writer's Life and Work

When Gabrielle Roy was born in Saint-Boniface, Manitoba, on 22 March 1909, she was the youngest of eleven children. But since the eight surviving children had already left home for school or work, "la petite dernière—the last little one," as she was affectionately called for a long time, felt very much like an "only child."[10] The childhood years of "enchantment" on Rue Deschambault were to be an unequaled period of "happiness, security and fascination with the unknown"[11] and have been so influential that Roy conjectures: "The sincerest images of my truest pages all come to me, I imagine, from that time."[12]

At first the great unknown was Winnipeg, Saint-Boniface's neighboring city. Immigrants of many nationalities gathered there before being dispersed throughout the West. The child was naturally fascinated by the strange sound of their language, their foreign dress and habits. How wonderful that the people and world of which her father used to talk should be so close at hand. As Léon Roy shared some of his experiences with his family, they seemed to meet in their very home "his" Little Ruthenians, "his" Dukhobors, "his" Mennonites, and all the other nationalities. In relating anecdotes of their daily lives and speaking with admiration of their industry and quest for freedom and pacificism, Léon Roy instilled in his youngest child a lasting interest in Canada's various ethnic groups. With gratitude Gabrielle Roy traces her compassion and acceptance of others to her childhood experiences. Perhaps it is not surprising, therefore, that she became Canada's most universal writer representing individuals of so many nationalities in her work, especially in her early journalistic articles, *Rue Deschambault* (*Street of Riches*, 1955), *Ces enfants dans ma vie* (*Children of my Heart*, 1977), and *Un jardin au bout du monde* (*Garden in the Wind*, 1975).

Thus Roy has been able, more than any other Canadian writer, to bridge the gap between the "two solitudes,"[13] i.e., between English and French Canadians, but also between the Canadian East and West. Beyond that she has become a spokesman for the Canadian mosaic to a larger extent than any other writer and ultimately addresses herself to an international public.

The Roys' respect for the cultural identities of Canada's immigrants was rooted in their attachment to Quebec, "the mother country."[14] "Quebec," Roy affirms, "was my undeniable past, my faith, my continuity, part of my soul, nostalgic, and maybe, incurable."[15] But the French-Canadians' endeavors to cultivate their linguistic heritage were not officially sanctioned by the provincial government of Manitoba. Thus two opposing worlds frequently conflicted with each other. "We worked in English and came home to French. We played in French, we prayed in French, we laughed in French, we wept in French."[16]

During Gabrielle's schooling at St. Joseph's Academy, with the Sisters of the Holy Names of Jesus and Mary (1915–1917), the most important subjects, "those that dealt with the soul, religion, our history,"[17] and French literature were taught in French; the rest were taught in English. The enrichment program that was aimed at preserving the French-Canadians' linguistic and cultural heritage presented certain risks to the teachers and called on their ingenuity because the teaching of French was not sanctioned by the province's Ministry of Education. The nuns' ingenuity in accommodating the English-speaking establishment and the Roman Catholic Church—two worlds apparently irreconcilable—is most vividly associated in Gabrielle Roy's memories when the classroom picture of the Archbishop had to be hastily exchanged for that of the Fathers of the Canadian Confederation, a switch that was apparently necessitated by the occasional English-speaking visitors whose expectations had to be met.

Books have of course always been influential for Gabrielle Roy. Of her schooldays she remembers "Thomas Hardy, George Eliot, Milton, Shakespeare, . . . Keats, Shelley, Coleridge."[18] Among Russian works Gogol's *Dead Souls* seemed familiar in light of her father's strange tales about "his" settlers. Similarly Roy discovered or, perhaps more appropriately, rediscovered in Chekhov's *The Steppe* a world resembling her own and a world that she associated particularly with her mother.

Daudet, Balzac, Proust, Colette, Mauriac, Bernanos, Camus, Montherlant, and Julien Green are but some of the French authors whose works she came to admire in later years. Among Scandinavian writers her favorites are Selma Lagerlöf and Sigrid Undset, Knut Hamsun and Par Lagerkvist; and among English writers she singles out Shakespeare, Virginia Woolf, Thomas Hardy, and the American, Thomas Wolfe.[19]

The theater—both French and English, especially Shakespeare—also had a profound influence on Gabrielle Roy during her formative years. She was an active member of Le Cercle Molière and participated with them in Canada's Dominion Drama Festival. As a result of her keen interest in the theater, she even considered acting as a career.

Léon Roy, who was forced to retire from his government post when his youngest was only four years old, died in 1927. Consequently Roy would soon be responsible for supporting herself and, partly, her mother. The young girl, still quite idealistic, resented the necessity of "earning a living." "To earn one's living! How mean it seemed to me, how selfish, how grasping!"[20] Echoes of Gabrielle Roy's youthful aspiration of becoming a writer or an artist, though transfigured, are apparent in "Gagner ma vie . . ." ("To Earn My Living . . ."), the final selection of *Rue Deschambault.*

Her studies at the Winnipeg Normal Institute (1927–1929) completed the young woman's formal schooling. In preparing herself for a teaching career, she followed in the footsteps of some of her sisters and fulfilled her mother's dream for her youngest. *La Petite Poule d'Eau* (*Where Nests the Water Hen,* 1950) and *Ces enfants de ma vie* (*Children of My Heart,* 1977) in particular were inspired by her experiences as a teacher.

After some eight years of teaching and despite her obvious success and fondness for children, however, Gabrielle Roy was not content to pursue that career. She found it difficult to justify even to herself her intention to leave home. Moreover, this decision was not readily understood and accepted by her mother and other members of her family. But the desire to respond to the unknown that took her to

Europe in 1937 was necessitated by introspection and the need to find herself and to be true to that self. The titular selection of *La Route d'Altamont* provides through Christine interesting insights into Roy's development at that time.

Her travels to Europe took her first to England. After six months of study at London's Guildhall School of Music and Drama, she realized that her future was not to be on the stage: "Acting is an interpretative art; I suppose that I prefer the creative one."[21]

Continuing her travels in France, Gabrielle Roy turned to writing to support herself. The mature writer she now is judges these beginnings of the late 1930s and early 1940s harshly. However, it is interesting to note that the sketches of life in England, France, and Canada, written for a number of magazines in France and Canada, already indicate characters and themes that would recur with greater force in her novels. More important, this occupation led to Roy's discovery that her writing responded to an irresistible creative urge.

When she began writing, she had to ask herself what language she should choose. Though completely bilingual, she soon decided to express herself in French, the language of her soul: "I think a writer speaks from his soul, and your soul is linked to one language more than another, even if you're familiar with several."[22]

On a deeper level Gabrielle Roy acknowledges another duality that has shaped her life and hence her work. The beauty of life always serves as a forceful reminder of the tragedy of life. This, she conjectures, may explain the "back-and-forth" of her books, i.e., after *"Bonheur d'occasion. . .*the book that has the most social implications. . .comes *La Petite Poule d'Eau* which seems to be almost the opposite."[23]

The decision to write in French also entailed her "return" to Canada and to Quebec rather than to Manitoba at the beginning of World War II: "I know now that without this return, I would not be the writer that I am today. I do not know what I would be without [the province of] Quebec. My debt to her [Quebec] is boundless. And at first, by having perceived in me a self that could not be recognized elsewhere, and by having seen it as perhaps no other gaze could have seen it, she [Quebec] made me know myself little by little and also know the essence of life, its torments and its joy."[24]

Initially upon her return to Canada, Gabrielle Roy took up residence in Montreal. Her journalistic assignments of the early forties focus on a series of articles on Montreal, the Abitibi and Gaspé regions, as well as sketches of Canada's ethnic minorities. Several of these essays and reports are included in *Fragiles lumières de la terre* (*The Fragile Lights of Earth,* 1978). The well-known critic Jean Ethier-Blais enthusiastically proclaims that this book, which he considers to be a "lesson in living," makes him "proud of being the contemporary of such a woman."[25] The combination of exact documentation and social and philosophical considerations was to be the ideal preparation for the future author of *Bonheur d'occasion* (*The Tin Flute,* 1945). As Paul Socken points out, these writings are "an illuminating companion to the novels. The three basic preoccupations that arise in the articles and short stories—the characters' understanding of themselves, their relationship to their environment, and their relationship to other characters—are shown more clearly in the novels to be interdependent."[26] At the same time, a desire to establish a sense of communication between the author and the reader, an anonymous person whose existence and approval she found she had to visualize in order to write, animated even these early beginnings. The concepts of communication with one's fellowmen and "a readiness, and openness for experience" are essential to understanding Gabrielle Roy's perception of her vocation as a writer.[27]

Her involuntary solitude in the metropolis, however, provided the more immediate impetus for the creation of her first novel. "The fundamental human need for a living warmth and the desire for affection and brotherly exchange led me in the right direction."[28]

The novelist's personal feelings for her characters transmit themselves in large measure to the reader of *Bonheur d'occasion*. Thus she emphasizes with the poverty-stricken Lacasse family whose misfortunes are compounded every year as the ever-increasing family is forced to ever poorer lodgings in one of Montreal's slum districts. How ironic that the war in Europe brings hope of relief from their misery, either through employment or enlistment.

The locale of Montreal links *Bonheur d'occasion* with *Alexandre Chenevert* (*The Cashier,* 1954). In the latter novel, however, Roy stresses to a far greater extent the fate of one man. In this portrait of a bank teller, tortured by his inability to shoulder the burdens of the world, the author succeeds in realizing the philosophy she would voice again in *La Montagne secrète* (*The Hidden Mountain,* 1961). "Every man is precious and unique by virtue of what life has made of him, or he of it. . . ."[29]

After her marriage to Dr. Marcel Carbotte in 1947, the couple spent two years in France. There her husband, also a native of Manitoba, pursued his medical studies in gynecology.

The idyllic *La Petite Poule d'Eau* (*Where Nests the Water Hen,* 1950) is based on Roy's experiences as a teacher and was written during that stay in France. This was the first of her "Manitoba" books that would alternate with those inspired by her more immediate surroundings.

Ces enfants de ma vie (*Children of My Heart,* 1977)—a fictionalized series of children's portraits by a young schoolteacher—is indicative of the lasting influence this period has had on Gabrielle Roy.

"Souvenirs du Manitoba" (1954), written "reluctantly"[30] in response to a request by the Royal Society of Canada, is of particular significance for the writer's development inasmuch as this essay marks the beginning of Roy's more autobiographical writings. Once she had overcome her initial reluctance in dealing with her formative years in Manitoba, Roy became engaged "in search of time lost, but above all—a quest of herself,"[31] as François Ricard terms it. Thus she soon discovered a flood of memories that found expression in a transposed form in *Rue Deschambault* (*Street of Riches,* 1955). As Ricard notes, therefore, the book is "as much a work of the imagination as a work of memory."[32]

Except for brief stays, Gabrielle Roy has not returned to Manitoba. Yet the prairie remains with her. In fact, over the years it has assumed increasing importance as a source of inspiration. Roy is truly a prairie writer as defined by the Canadian critic Eli Mandel: ". . . it isn't place that we have to talk about, but something more complicated and more compelling: remembered place or—beyond that—remembered self, something lost and recovered, a kind of memory, a kind of myth."[33]

Roy herself acknowledges that even more important than the physical impact of the landscape is the symbolic value she associates with it. The prairie horizon, "endlessly calling, endlessly slipping away, is perhaps the symbol, the image in our lives of the ideal, or of the future, which appears to us, when we are young, to be a generous source of ever abundant and renewed promises."[34] It will be seen that such correspondence between the landscape and man is a characteristic feature of Gabrielle Roy's work.

In 1954, after a second two-year stay in France, the Carbottes took up permanent residence in Quebec City. There Roy leads a life devoted almost exclusively to her art, an exacting task. This is possible partly because the couple have no children. In this regard the novelist notes: "As a young woman, I did desire them. But after a few books I saw they were a gift equivalent [*sic*]."[35] However satisfying writing may be, it imposes many sacrifices. In this regard, as our discussion will bear out, *La Montagne secrète* (*The Hidden Mountain,* 1961), the fictionalized biography of a painter, provides significant insights. While she readily accepts Wordsworth's idea that art is emotion recollected in tranquility, Roy does not think ". . . that any work of art or of a creative sort is done in a state of relaxation."[36] Privacy is, therefore, essential for the artist. Gabrielle Roy, we recall, submitted reluctantly and only briefly to the demands the public made on her as a result of the international acclaim of *Bonheur d'occasion.*

She recognizes, of course, the paradox between her isolation as an artist and the desire for communion and communication that inspires her to write. At the same time she feels she can separate herself from man to write because man is within her.

In light of Gabrielle Roy's commitment to man, it is fitting that she should have become a spokesman for Montreal's Expo '67 and "Terre des hommes/Man and His World," a symbolic manifestation of faith in man and progress.

True to the spirit of "Terre des Hommes" and Antoine de Saint-Exupéry whose faith in the family of man is a continuing inspiration, Roy justly assesses her achievements as a writer in these terms: "My merit, if I dare pretend to any, is perhaps to have assembled in my books beings so separate and scattered who, nevertheless, still constitute one family."[37]

With Gabrielle Roy's death of a heart attack on 13 July 1983, Canada has lost one of its most talented and best loved authors. Her death brings to mind her comparative reflections on the fleeting nature of people's lives and fireflies in *Cet été qui chantait* (*Enchanted Summer,* 1972). Although her loss is great, we may take comfort in the thought that she was among those "who before they are extinguished shine with their full light. Caught in God's fire."[38] And thus the author of *Fragiles lumières de la terre* will continue to enrich her readers.

Chapter Two
The Urban Novels

In 1961, in an interview with Judith Jasmin, Gabrielle Roy spoke of two polarities in her work: first, an interest in the common people and everyday, contemporary life, and second, an interest in herself, in discovering herself. Initially these two interests in her writings entail an oscillation between the city and the prairie countryside or, in the words of Alan Brown, "a dialogue of experience and innocence."[1] More recently, however, the more personal mode predominates. For the purpose of this discussion, *Bonheur d'occasion (The Tin Flute,* 1945) and *Alexandre Chenevert (The Cashier,* 1954), both set in Montreal, will be grouped together.

Despite considerable similarities and a common inspiration, *Bonheur d'occasion* and *Alexandre Chenevert* are separate works whose individuality brings to mind Paul Bourget's differentiation between the novel of customs and manners *(le roman de moeurs)* and the novel of character *(le roman de caractère).* The plot is more developed in *Bonheur d'occasion* which depicts average people engaged in familiar activities, while *Alexandre Chenevert* portrays in a more analytical manner a complex, exceptional individual.

Bonheur d'occasion

In the context of French-Canadian literature *Bonheur d'occasion (The Tin Flute)* breaks new ground. As Gabrielle Roy observed in 1947: "We [French-Canadians] are forgetting to be afraid of ourselves and getting away from the habit of imitating others. We are getting down to our own truth and to our own experience."[2] It was an endeavor with fortunate results, as it allowed the author to reach readers well beyond provincial confines. David M. Hayne, for example, suggests: "For perhaps the first time, a Montreal novel illustrates, in Montreal terms, human situations which exist in great cities everywhere. . . . The great achievement of Gabrielle Roy in *Bonheur d'occasion* is to have taken a simple human situation and to have presented it in French-Canadian terms without sacrificing anything of its

universal interest."[3] Pierre Descaves also praises Gabrielle Roy for offering the European reader a new image of Canada.[4] Similarly the
French critic Francis Ambrière suggests that *Bonheur d'occasion* is most
noteworthy for its "universal meaning,"[5] a sentiment that is echoed
also by H. Gueux-Rolle.[6] While Hugo McPherson justly attributes
the success of *Bonheur d'occasion* essentially to "its stunning documen-
tary quality,"[7] it clearly bears the stamp of its author which leads to
Guy Sylvestre's conclusion that *Bonheur d'occasion* may well be French-
Canada's "most human novel."[8] William Arthur Deacon discerns a
touch of Flaubert in Gabrielle Roy's descriptions: "The exquisite care
of every homely detail, giving concrete reality to a stick of cheap fur-
niture, to the drifting snow, to the taxi-driver's grandiose talk, is
what this French master [Flaubert] seems to have taught his apt pupil
in Canada. Everything in *The Tin Flute,* and every person, is unre-
markable, yet the patience, the skill of phrasing, of steering the story
from point to point, gives this novel power that captivates the imagination of readers. . . . This makes the book a work of art."[9] "A perfect example of naturalism, a work of art which is at the same time
an accurate case-history of social disease, poverty," as W. E. Colin
terms it, Gabrielle Roy's novel "owes nothing to the main determi-
nants of French-Canadian literature. It continues a nineteenth century
French tradition and as a work of art it depends solely on its perfection as an experimental novel."[10] We do not imply that Roy has attained the stature of a Stendhal or a Balzac. Nevertheless, we do
recognize with pleasure the traditional qualities of "warmth, compassion, and humanity" which Doris Lessing, who deplores their absence
in much contemporary writing, believes made the greatest novels of
the past "a statement of faith in man himself."[11]

As W. B. Thorne has pointed out, *Bonheur d'occasion* is "the odyssey of a people victimized by a society dedicated mainly to the pursuit of happiness only of the 'haves.' "[12] The original title, as Hugo
McPherson notes, suggests " 'chance' happiness, 'grab-bag' happiness, and 'bargain' happiness—a deceptive, fleeting joy."[13] The English title, *The Tin Flute,* may be considered more pessimistic because
it focuses attention on the denial rather than the fulfillment of a
child's dream. Yet this was inevitable during the Depression when
the struggle for survival, in a literal sense, was a daily preoccupation.
The consciousness of these tragic lives might well incite a writer's
bitterness or cruelty. But not in Gabrielle Roy, for we recognize in

her "the anguished heart" which she admired in her fellow writer Germaine Guèvremont. [14]

Bonheur d'occasion was a deeply personal experience in its conception and creative composition. More than a story, it is a testimony of Gabrielle Roy's vision of life and attitude toward truth. Looking back on her first novel in later years, Roy interprets this work not only as a mirror of Montreal at that time, but also as a testimony of the vision of life and attitude toward truth by which she lived in the early 1940s.

Having come to Montreal from the Canadian prairies via France, Gabrielle Roy decided to explore her new surroundings in an effort to overcome a feeling of intense loneliness. The beauty of nature's rebirth in spring even in the metropolis of Montreal clashed with the hopelessness of the lives of its poorest inhabitants. Indignation prompted the idealistic young writer to arouse in her readers a kindred consciousness of these people's plight in an endeavor to change their lives.

Roy's vision of 1939 owes its origin directly to her world. Almost inexplicably and somewhat reluctantly she found herself with a major work of fiction on her hands. Conceived initially as a short story, however, *Bonheur d'occasion* soon developed into her first novel whose composition occupied her for approximately four years.

To be able to share one's vision, Roy insists, the artist "retiring to a shell"[15] must devote himself to a long and laborious task. In this creative process simplification and concentration of the "realistic foundation"[16] are essential if a work of art is to be achieved.

The artist, however, is not always in full control of his material: "I still think sometimes of characters that I have created as people with an autonomy of their own," Roy observes. [17] This probably explains the absence of a distinct protagonist in *Bonheur d'occasion,* unless the district of Saint-Henri itself be seen as such, as B. Lafleur suggests. [18] As Roy re-creates in chronological order the life of Saint-Henri, a railway factory slum along the Lachine Canal in Montreal, as exemplified by the fortunes of the Lacasse family, Florentine Lacasse and her mother Rose-Anna seem to be rivals for the reader's attention.

It is interesting to note that while writing the novel, Gabrielle Roy saw Saint-Henri essentially in terms of the regional, rather than the universal aspect of her milieu. Her contemporary French-Cana-

dian critics similarly tended to focus on the novel's regionalism. Un-
accustomed as they were to such an unflattering "social frescoe,"[19]
Gabrielle Roy's stark realism naturally, though unjustly, provoked
occasional negative reaction. As already indicated, European, English
Canadian, and American critics, by contrast, have always been impressed by the universal aspect of *Bonheur d'occasion*. While time and
action are detailed, the human misery that the novel portrays is
timeless and reminds the reader of the world's increasing interrelation
and unity.

The regional aspect of *Bonheur d'occasion* is reinforced also by the
novelist's frequent use of dialogue that faithfully reproduces the district's dialect and anglicisms.

The story of *Bonheur d'occasion*, as Réjan Robidoux and André Renaud indicate in their analysis, develops on a threefold level: that of
the individual, the social, and the global.[20]

On an individual level *Bonheur d'occasion* is the story of Florentine.
The eldest of the Lacasse children, she is a waitress in the restaurant
of a five-and-ten-cent store. Almost all her wages go toward supporting her family. Intent on escaping the poverty she has known all her
life and yearning for happiness on her own terms, Florentine naively
succumbs to the charms of the ambitious Jean Lévesque. Jean and
Florentine strongly resemble each other in their aspirations and striv-
ings for a brighter future. Ironically, however, in Jean's opinion at
least, the social background they share presents an obstacle to their
common goal. He soon realizes that the young woman represents the
essence of everything from which he wants to free himself. Moreover,
he is convinced that in the difficult struggle ahead of him, he must
be alone. Their affair is abruptly broken off when he learns of her
pregnancy. Florentine then decides to marry Emmanuel Letourneau,
Jean Lévesque's friend, who is totally ignorant of her deceit.

Rose-Anna, the mother, is the center of the social level. She is also
the moral mainstay of her family, whose breakup, however, she cannot prevent. This gentle, warm-hearted woman somewhat reluctantly
assumes the role of the head of the household, a role for which her
husband Azarius, the eternal dreamer, is unfit.

Idealized memories of her childhood and youth are the focus of
Rose-Anna's dreams of happiness. But her escape to the past is cruelly
embittered when Azarius fulfills her dreams of taking her to her
childhood home again. The ill-fated excursion to Rose-Anna's former

country home allows Gabrielle Roy to fuse the individual, the social, and the global levels.

Florentine refuses to join the family excursion so that she may invite Jean Lévesque to her home during her parents' absence. In retrospect she realizes that this incident is the very cause of their ultimate separation since it is at this time that she becomes pregnant.

Rose-Anna is forced to recognize that "you cannot go home again." She is deceived not only by the colors, sounds, and scenes of the past, but also by the starkness of her family's present poverty. Her impotence against forces beyond her control is impressed upon her as she sees the contrast between her children and their more prosperous country cousins. Azarius imposes even greater hardships on the family when once again he loses his job due to an accident on their return to the city (he had taken a truck without permission) and eventually goes overseas to Europe as a soldier.

Expanding her focus to the international level, Gabrielle Roy reveals how the advent of World War II promises the poor of Saint-Henri unexpected prosperity. They may either take advantage of employment opportunities, like Jean Lévesque who works in an ammunition factory, or enlist in the army, like several members of the Lacasse family.

Roy's involvement in the lives of her fictional characters becomes frequently so intense that they continue to preoccupy her even after she has completed a given book. This happened with *Bonheur d'occasion*. Thus, when she was honored by the Royal Society of Canada in 1947 for her successful first novel, she chose to speak once again about the characters of *Bonheur d'occasion*. In "Retour à Saint-Henri" ("Return to Saint-Henri"), as she entitled her Reception Speech to the Royal Society of Canada, her audience shared in Roy's imaginary visit to the setting of *Bonheur d'occasion*. This revealing encounter with her fictional characters provides a remarkable example of cogent criticism, as will become evident later in the character analysis. In light of the writer's aforementioned concern with the plight of the people who had inspired her to write *Bonheur d'occasion* and her expectation that her readers would be similarly indignant and therefore effect changes, the reader understands Gabrielle Roy's "sense of futility"[21] upon discovering Saint-Henri unchanged.

Gabrielle Roy's sense of personal involvement also plays a major role in the portrayal of her characters. It is most appropriate that at the very beginning of *Bonheur d'occasion* the reader should meet Florentine Lacasse at the restaurant counter of the five-and-ten-cent store where she works. The atmosphere that is established through the detailed description of the restaurant's bustling activity and the faithful transcription of the customers' talk is reminiscent of Roy's objective journalistic technique. At the same time the establishing of the ambiance is typical of a pattern by which the novelist introduces her characters whose identities are essentially derived from their environment. The "pathetic fallacy," as Gérard Bessette and André Brochu, for example, have pointed out, plays a major role in *Bonheur d'occasion*.[22]

Both milieu and time are formidable enemies. "For her [Florentine] this place summed up the pinched, hurried, restless character of her whole life in Saint-Henri."[23] The waitress's future seems predestined. Florentine foresees only a repetition of the experience of the past. Practically each year is marked by yet another move to a more wretched "home," hardly worthy of that name. But she cannot resign herself to such a fatalistic existence. Instead, a spirit of conscious and unconscious revolt against a woman's fate, as exemplified by her mother, guides her behavior. The reader has to await *Rue Deschambault* (*Street of Riches,* 1955) and *La Route d'Altamont* (*The Road Past Altamont,* 1966) to see a more positive example of successive generations becoming reconciled to their lives.

When Florentine realizes that Jean refuses to tie himself to her, she has reached a turning point in her life. "Her dreams were dead. Her youth was dead."[24] Luckily, however, Emmanuel Letourneau, who yearns for companionship and love, turns to Florentine. The very things that repel Jean, attract Emmanuel to Florentine. But his love does not blind him: "Refined! Was Florentine refined? No. She was more like a street urchin, with crude turns of speech and vulgar manners. She was better than refined, she was life itself, with her knowledge of poverty and her revolt against poverty."[25] Ruthlessly Florentine enters into a loveless and uneventful marriage with Emmanuel. She would no longer experience the thrill of the unknown that had attracted and repelled her at the same time, promising both the greatest joy and the greatest sorrow.

As Emmanuel leaves for the front, the egocentric Florentine shows little concern for his welfare. She experiences a certain satisfaction in knowing that she had not been defeated by recent events and has confidence in the future.

After Gabrielle Roy "returned" to Saint-Henri (as the author termed it in her Reception Speech to the Royal Society of Canada in 1947), she noted that Florentine was difficult to recognize now, for hers was "the face of thousands of women."[26] While she had progressed socially and economically, she also appeared less attractive—much more like the ambitious Jean Lévesque than the idealistic Emmanuel.

Jean Lévesque is essentially Florentine's male counterpart. The machinist's ambivalent feelings for her are rooted in their common origin. This becomes dramatically clear to him moments before their lovemaking:

> He knew now what it was that Florentine's home reminded him of, the thing he had feared above all: the smell of poverty, the powerful smell of cheap, well-worn clothes, a smell he would recognize blindfolded. And he realized that Florentine herself stood for the kind of poverty against which his whole soul rebelled. At the same time he understood the attraction she had for him. She was his poverty, his solitude, his dreary childhood, his lonely youth; she was everything he had hated and denied; she was what lay at the root of his character.[27]

Absolute independence, Jean Lévesque firmly believes, is essential for him if his ambitions are to be realized. Seeking through his labors to revenge himself on the world for his humble origins, he despises himself for his brief interest in this woman, as he falls short of the ruthless personality he is intent on forging for himself.

For Jean Lévesque the conviction of future success, entailing social and monetary rewards, adequately compensates him for the sacrifices he feels he must impose upon himself at present. But in his efforts to create a new self of his own making, he must suppress some of the very qualities he unconsciously yearns for, but consciously regards as weakness. Like Florentine, he considers the essence of his humanity negatively. Inasmuch as this perception extends also to his fellow-men, he is as harsh toward others as he is to himself, as seen, for example, by his desertion of the woman who is expecting his child.

Anticipating her imaginary meeting with Lévesque after the war, Roy notes: "Jean Lévesque, . . . in whom I personified the rejection of social responsibility and the egotism of those who accept the advantages of society without giving up any scrap of personal liberty in return, certainly is taking full advantage of the conditions of present-

day life. . . . I could never follow him through his life. The Jean
Lévesques are so numerous among us."[28]

In contrast to the selfish Jean and Florentine, Rose-Anna devotes
herself to her large family. "Humility and the strength of tenderness"
are the distinguishing features of that remarkable woman who is also
representative of universal motherhood. "This little working-class
woman, gentle and imaginative—I can admit this to you today," Roy
declared to the members of the Royal Society of Canada, "almost
forced her way into my story, then turned the plot upside down and,
finally, managed to dominate the book through her very unliterary
quality of tenderness. . . . without the humility and strength of her
tenderness I doubt that my story would have had the gift of touching
the heart. It is only by sacrificing ourselves to someone or to some
higher goal that a life can move others."[29]

Roy acknowledges that Rose-Anna—and Emmanuel—are espe-
cially dear to her. "I have loved all the characters in *The Tin Flute*. I
cannot conceive how a novelist could fail to pity or love the smallest
creation of his imagination; incomplete as these characters may be,
they are the writer's bond with the real world, its suffering and heart-
break. But as time goes by I notice that two of my characters console
me for the others, . . . Because both of them lived for the good of
others, Emmanuel and Rose-Anna leave us perhaps not quite deprived of hope."[30]

The fact that Rose-Anna "forced her way into [her] story" (as Roy
acknowledged)[31] probably accounts for a certain malaise some critics,
including André Brochu[32] and Gérard Bessette,[33] have felt as to the
relative importance of Rose-Anna and Florentine. Nevertheless, these
critics praise most highly these women's characterizations. Bessette,
for example, even compares Roy's heroines of *Bonheur d'occasion* with
those of Zola, Dostoevski, and George Eliot. From a structural point
of view, the novelist focuses on Florentine, both at the beginning and
at the end of *Bonheur d'occasion*. Yet the difference between mother
and daughter is such that despite the equally successful characterizations, the author's and, hence, the reader's sympathies shift to the
older woman.

Rose-Anna's marriage to Azarius Lacasse led to her move to the
city and a life of increasing poverty. Without ill will, though against
her natural inclination, the resourceful woman assumes the role of
leadership whenever necessary. At the same time her love sensitizes
her to her husband's feelings.

Believing that misery is part of the human condition—and especially a woman's lot, since she lacks a man's independence—Rose-Anna treasures her childhood memories. Ironically, while her fortitude and daily heroism have alleviated their misery in their squalid surroundings, her zest for living and hope seem ineffectual, even misplaced, when she returns to her former country home. Although Rose-Anna does not believe in Azarius's dreams, she is too proud and loyal to reveal the truth to her mother. But the disparity between reality and what she would have her mother believe is all too obvious.

Rose-Anna's humiliation, in turn, encourages criticism of her mother and reinforces the lack of communication between them. At the same time Rose-Anna justly fears that she may fail Florentine. Indeed, Rose-Anna's love cannot prevent the breakup of the family, for their individual dreams of happiness are all rooted in longing to escape their home, whose wretchedness and narrow confines seem less a haven than a prison.

As an incurable dreamer, Azarius Lacasse had always been making great plans as if he were free to choose his destiny. The superficiality of his character is emphasized by the fact that the author concentrates on portraying him from the outside rather than the inside. In contrast to the praise that her characterization of women has generally earned for her, Roy appears to be less successful in portraying male characters. Gérard Bessette is particularly critical. "Gabrielle Roy seems incapable of portraying a complex, fully developed male character."[34]

"An idealist, a ne'er-do-well," is Jean Lévesque's just assessment of Azarius and he condemns the older man for denying his family a feeling of security. But Azarius, as Rose-Anna especially acknowledges, is also kind and generous. "He never had much luck,"[35] Florentine concludes, when she describes her family to Emmanuel. But "luck" presents itself to the unemployed carpenter in the guise of a soldier's uniform. His proposed enlistment is to prove his love for Rose-Anna. Nevertheless, he thinks more of himself and the burden that family ties present for him. Enlisting is a means of escape, "the guarantee of his own freedom. He was free, free, incredibly free; he was going to begin life all over again."[36]

Renewing her acquaintance with Azarius after the war, Gabrielle Roy finds him not at his carpentry trade, but driving a taxi. He has changed little and remains the perpetual dreamer.

Emmanuel Letourneau, too, is an idealist and a dreamer. But

whereas the older man escapes through his dreams from his obliga-
tions, Emmanuel assumes responsibilities and sacrifices. Also, like
the cashier, the protagonist in *Alexandre Chenevert,* Emmanuel aspires
to universal brotherhood. His actions, however, are more effective
than Chenevert's because the young soldier is more realistic regarding
his abilities. Emmanuel's home is now in Montreal's prestigious
Westmount district. His roots, however, are in Saint-Henri. Despite
a college education and the foremanship in a cotton mill, he has not
forgotten his former schoolmates and the hopelessness of their daily
existence. But Roy does not relate how Emmanuel's parents were able
to overcome their humble background and make their home in Westmount. And the isolated example of the Letourneaus' change of for-
tune does not attenuate the tragic atmosphere of *Bonheur d'occasion.*

Roy envisages for Emmanuel, who like Rose-Anna is especially
dear to her (as noted above), basically a tragic existence. Unlike Jean
Lévesque, Emmanuel does not profit from his favorable economic environment. Ironically, his idealism isolates, even alienates, him from
the very persons he wants to help. Thus the novelist notes in "Return
to Saint-Henri," her Reception Speech to the Royal Society of Canada: "I must admit I haven't the courage to bring him [Emmanuel]
back, he who, at the outbreak of war, walked one night up Westmount hill to ask the wealthy houses if they would not like to add
their sacrifice for the sake of peace. . . . Emmanuel is dead. He was
the spirit of rebellious youth that will settle for nothing less than perfect justice, and thus was marked for sacrifice."[37]

"Life, in Gabrielle Roy's world, is never static," writes Paul
Socken. "It represents a continuing process of change which renders
the quest for bonheur/joie difficult but not impossible."[38] In light of
the emptiness and dreariness of their daily lives, the search for happiness almost inevitably takes a form of escape for many of her characters. A particularly poignant example of the apparent futility of this
innate yearning is that of Daniel Lacasse. Rose-Anna's resolve to fulfill the child's wish for a flute, however, remains only a good intention. Yet when Rose-Anna visits Daniel, who suffers from leukemia,
in the hospital and finds him with the little tin flute and more toys
than he could ever have wished for, the grief-stricken mother knows
that such joys have come too late for the dying boy.

For Daniel's sister Yvonne, religious mysticism offers another ave-
nue of escape from the sordidness surrounding her. Much like Emmanuel, she is alone, concerned with shouldering the sins of her

fellowmen and preoccupied with the meaning of man's existence and eternal life. Yvonne thus follows a path that alienates her from her family who cannot share the depth of her faith.

For others, happiness, or at least the promise of happiness, presents itself in the guise of war. Thus Eugène Lacasse is one of the first to enlist. His decision is based on economic conditions rather than on idealism. War in a distant land represents employment, a measure of economic security, and freedom. But Eugène is too much the son of Azarius Lacasse not to embellish before long his egoistic motivation. Soon he believes himself completely altruistic.

The diverse reactions to war expressed in *Bonheur d'occasion* emphasize the complexity of the society Roy portrays and are an important aspect of her realism. For the ambitious and practical Florentine Lacasse, enlisting is easily explained. Selfish desires and considerations and personal gains motivate all men, she tells the disillusioned Emmanuel, whose sense of alienation and despair regarding society is only heightened by such a cynical response. The peace-loving Rose-Anna sympathizes with women everywhere whose loved ones are engaged in war. As news from the fronts incites more men to enlist, she comes to hate the Germans rather than the war itself. At the same time this hatred troubles her, for she realizes that such a feeling can only aggravate hostilities. Eugène and Azarius Lacasse readily defend the idea of the war. Jean Lévesque is intent on obtaining the greatest possible personal gains, though he recognizes that on both sides the soldiers are probably fighting for the same ideals. Such consideration of the common—or at least parallel—commitment to one's country, wherever it may be, raises doubts in Emmanuel Letourneau as war, paradoxically, fosters the concept of universal brotherhood.

Roy's vision of the individual, social, and global levels, as represented in *Bonheur d'occasion,* is evidently marked by strong tragic overtones. Internal and external forces threaten not only the harmonious development, but at times even the very existence of the characters whose lives she reveals. While Florentine Lacasse and Jean Lévesque may appear to prosper on the individual level, they suppress at the same time their most humane traits in a hostile environment. The selflessness of Rose-Anna Lacasse and of Emanuel Letourneau, on the other hand, who represent primarily the social and global levels respectively, ultimately cannot prevail against the destruction of the family or motivate others to share their ideal of the brotherhood of man. Yet it is significant that Roy in her innermost being rebels against the negative vision of *Bonheur d'occasion*, however realistic it may be.

Thus she creates in *La Petite Poule d'Eau (Where Nests the Water Hen)* and *Alexandre Chenevert (The Cashier)* once again the types of character that preoccupy her and that are dearest to her. With Luzina Tousignant, therefore, she imagines the kind of family life that Rose-Anna might have created in a more favorable environment. And the focus on Alexandre Chenevert allows Roy to develop in depth the global concerns of Emmanuel that were in *Bonheur d'occasion* necessarily frequently understood rather than explained. But the joy of *La Petite Poule d'Eau*, the work that succeeded *Bonheur d'occasion*, contrasts again sharply with the later *Alexandre Chenevert*.

Alexandre Chenevert

Gabrielle Roy admirably demonstrates in *Alexandre Chenevert (The Cashier)*, a "classic of empathy,"[39] in the words of W. C. Lougheed, the qualities that Joseph Conrad identifies with the serious artist: "In his dealings with mankind, he should be capable of giving a tender recognition of their obscure virtues."[40]

The psychological insights for which Roy was justly praised after *Bonheur d'occasion* are even more apparent and important in *Alexandre Chenevert*, "a remarkable book, remarkable for its truth and its quiet, unsensational power," in the words of Elizabeth Janeway.[41] Margaret A. Heidemann also notes that "this is a novel of distinction and integrity which displays the deepening insights and broader scope, the advance in accomplishment which the previous work of this author had promised,"[42] and Gérard Tougas[43] considers it to be Roy's best work. And the acclaimed novelist Andrée Maillet is similarly unsparing in her praise of this novel by a "a great artist" from whom she has much to learn.[44] The French critic Firmin Roz likewise suggests that *Alexandre Chenevert*, whose form and content are on an equally high level, ranks among the best works of French literature.[45] Like Maillet, Roz also stresses the universality and timelessness that paradoxically owes its origins to the exact "local and timely truths."

Gabrielle Roy first contemplated writing the story of "the little man," a postwar characterization of a "Salavin," as R. M. Desnues suggests,[46] between 1947 and 1950 while with her husband in Paris. Roy's portrait of modern man, like that of Georges Duhamel, arouses the reader's pity and aversion at the same time, and both novelists reveal exceptional empathy for their protagonists. Yet it would be wrong to suggest that Roy, whose portrait of her strange hero mirrors the Canadian reality, has been influenced by Duhamel. Before finalizing her portrait of the Canadian cashier, however, she developed in three short stories the life of a white-collar worker obsessed by financial worries and isolated from his family.[47] Alexandre Chenevert is indeed on one level "legion,"[48] i.e., a man whose hectic lifestyle may be seen in hundreds and thousands of lives surrounding us and disappearing in the anonymous multitude. Thus Roy could still say in 1979, some twenty-five years after the publication of her novel, that Alexandre Chenevert still pursues her, pleading with her not to turn a blind eye to the world's suffering but to reveal it for her readers.[49]

In refining her technique, Roy shifts her attention from the masses to the individual, which allows "full scope for her unequalled gifts as clinical examiner of the human heart."[50] This entails also a considerably heightened sense of tragedy, for, whereas in *Bonheur d'occasion* the milieu is largely perceived as an imprisoning force, Alexandre Chenevert is a prisoner of his self. This is skillfully demonstrated by the novelist's use of the bank teller's cage in a literal and a symbolic sense. Also, the plot becomes almost insignificant, partly due to the protagonist's life, or, one might rather say, his death. Lastly, on the stylistic level, there are fewer uses of regional terms and anglicisms than in *Bonheur d'occasion*.

Part 1 of three parts of *Alexandre Chenevert* deals with a middle-aged bank teller's daily existence in all its monotonous detail in Montreal in the late 1940s. "In all, a powerful description of a weak man," S. G. Perry observes.[51] Frustrated by the apparent impersonality of his urban milieu, Alexandre Chenevert aspires to rise above the anonymous multitude. In his warped mind even sickness has a certain appeal. "I'll end by dying of cancer of the stomach, Alexandre told himself with a certain archness, as though he would thus at least attain a fate wholly his own."[52] But when his wife falls ill, he resents her brief hospitalization since it involves unexpected expenses. The teller's awareness of the misery throughout the world increases both his sense of helplessness and his feeling of alienation from his fellow-men who not only seem indifferent to the fate of others, but even to enjoy life. Ironically Chenevert's discontent with himself and the world renders him incapable of recognizing people's goodwill toward him and others on a small, but more realistic scale and prevents him from expressing friendship or love for his co-workers and those closest to him. At the same time the overly conscientious Chenevert lacks all sense of proportion, so that a loose overcoat button torments his overactive mind as much as the threat of the atomic bomb does. Similarly, although he suffers from ill health, he contemplates emulating Mahatma Gandhi in his hunger strike to show his sympathy for that great humanitarian.

A $100 mistake in balancing his books, which results in his having to work overtime to make up the apparent loss, further affects Chenevert's ill health. Yet when the money is recovered, his tortured mind still finds no relief. Finally a doctor, who realizes that the teller's stomach problems are essentially caused by his trying to shoulder the world's problems, persuades him to take a holiday.

Part 2 takes Alexandre Chenevert to the Laurentian Mountains only a few miles from Montreal. At Lac Vert he discovers in the LeGardeurs for the first time "human beings admitting to happiness."[53] These farmers have found contentment in the mere satisfaction of their simplest needs through the labor of their own hands. Tragically their willingness to share their life with the stranger from the city, manifesting a true spirit of brotherly love, is incomprehensible to the very man whose yearning to devote himself to others remains on an abstract level. Totally ignorant of the natural hardships his hosts often face and of his own inability to live off the land, a happy Alexandre Chenevert writes to his wife of his plans for a better life in the country (in a letter he will never mail). But the teller's serenity is short-lived. Anticipating the work that awaits him, he breaks off his brief holiday. As he approaches the city, however, he is once again so overwhelmed by its ugliness and indifference that his wife justly concludes that his holiday has not benefited him at all.

Part 3 relates the agony of Chenevert's slow death from cancer. At the same time he experiences a kind of conversion on the human and spiritual level that reconciles him at last to his fellowmen and God. Thus, as Robert Weaver enthusiastically notes: "Chenevert's death and triumph are simply the fitting climax of a beautifully proportioned work of fiction by a writer who must be regarded as one of our most ambitious and admirable novelists."[54]

In choosing such a pathetic figure as Alexandre Chenevert as her protagonist, Gabrielle Roy obviously has taken up a major challenge. "It takes art," as Margaret A. Heidemann affirms, "to make such a depressing character so sympathetic that the reader follows his almost plotless progress with absorption."[55] In contrast to the general praise, however, reserved for *Alexandre Chenevert,* Gilles Marcotte maintains that "Alexandre Chenevert remains a theme, rather than a man."[56] Far from portraying the teller "as one would like him to be,"[57] Roy reveals him with all his weaknesses. This has called forth some criticism. But the author defends the necessity of Chenevert's strange character: "Alexandre, many people considered to be insane in his excess of sensitivity, but he had to be sensitive in order to be the filter or the sounding board of the discrepancies of our time."[58] Thus the reader alternates at times between annoyance and sympathy not only because Chenevert's misery to a certain extent is self-induced, but also because the reader recognizes that he, too, is somewhat like the bank teller Chenevert.

At first Alexandre Chenevert appears to be Everyman. The impression of his anonymity among the masses of a metropolis is accentuated further by the novel's English title—*The Cashier.* Yet gradually the "little man" reveals his individuality. Thus Roy reverses the usual fictional process of creating an individual who eventually becomes a type. Elizabeth Janeway, in particular, praises Roy for this approach. "Here is Mlle Roy's achievement—though Alexandre suffers what every man suffers, he is not Everyman. He is not a hollow symbol but a differentiated human being and thus the proper subject of fiction."[59]

Eugénie Chenevert readily admits that her husband has "fine qualities," but she also acknowledges that traits such as his prudence, honesty, and lack of diplomacy, by their very excess, make life more difficult for everyone. A man of profound contradictions, he dreams of universal brotherhood, but appears cold and distant even to his wife and daughter, as well as his fellowworkers and customers.

Occasionally Roy grants her protagonist a realistic perception of his own misanthropic character. Yet, much as in *Bonheur d'occasion,* a sense of fatalism interferes. Thus Chenevert, like most of mankind, profits little from his own or others' experiences. Inevitably his resolutions to wholly change his life come to nothing.

Just as the lives of the people of Saint-Henri in *Bonheur d'occasion* were disrupted by world events, Chenevert presents a vivid reminder that no man is an island. But there is a significant difference. Chenevert believes himself to be a world citizen and, in contrast to the Lacasses, voluntarily seeks to become involved in the lives of his fellowmen. Like Emmanuel Letourneau in *Bonheur d'occasion,* Chenevert feels diminished in his humanity if he fails to struggle against misfortune.

Attempting to shoulder the burdens of the world, the would-be Atlas is physically unfit for such a task. Indeed, his concern for others contributes in part to his ill health. Though Alexandre Chenevert may be a model bank employee, his scrupulosity gives him little satisfaction in his relationship with his fellow employees or with life in general. His increasing ill health deepens his sense of alienation.

In this novel the alienation is even greater and more tragic than that which contributes to the breakup of the family in *Bonheur d'occasion*. The bank teller is as much a stranger in Montreal as he would be in any city, for he is fundamentally a stranger to himself. Chenevert is alone and believes that his isolation is largely inherent in city life. "His longing for a desert island"[60] in the metropolis and his need at Lac Vert for the city, whose life suddenly seems to represent a constant fraternal exchange, are but more examples of the cashier's contradictory personality.

In a moment of self-recognition Alexandre Chenevert "saw himself in his own heart just as he must appear in the eyes of others: a sharp, conscientious man whom he, the very first of all, would have found intolerable." Though he is shocked at the realization that he is "so much a stranger to himself and even an enemy,"[61] Alexandre cannot profit from this realization. For, inasmuch as he attributes his failure to be himself to his milieu rather than to his personal attitudes, development is denied to him. A disillusioned Eugénie Chenevert sadly concludes on the eve of her husband's death that she is losing a man who was never really what he could have been.

Alexandre's alienation is also related to his concept of time and space. Invariably the unhappy man lives, or tries to live, by denying, frequently unconsciously, the present. Regretting the past, not because of a nostalgic sense of wasted happiness, but rather because of lost opportunities, he centers his expectations on the coming day. Yet the future seems to foreshadow ever greater misfortunes, especially on a global scale. Only at Lac Vert, when he is momentarily released from himself, does he gratefully enjoy the freedom of being completely oblivious of the past and, even, of the future.

Similarly Chenevert sees his confining physical milieu as an inhibiting factor to self-realization. The Cheneverts' city apartment provides no real privacy, and their neighbors are perceived as potential enemies or at least as strangers. At work Alexandre Chenevert is surrounded by a glass cage. While he must work there, he resents it; yet during his short vacation and even more so when he lies on his deathbed, the cashier yearns to return to his cage in the bank which now represents an ideal of "human solidarity."[62]

It would be wrong to assume that Gabrielle Roy suggests that modern man's problems lie essentially in alienating city milieus. Though Roy's second novel, *La Petite Poule d'Eau* (the novel that preceded *Alexandre Chenevert*) presents us with the example of an idealized pastoral existence, it is not to be regarded as a general model. In *Bonheur d'occasion* we recall that Rose-Anna's expectations on her return to her childhood home are cruelly deceived. But, as long as Alexandre Chenevert is not in harmony with himself, he cannot be in harmony with others and his surroundings. Thus Chenevert, a prisoner of his self, finds the cottage at Lac Vert too small inside, but the landscape overwhelming in its vastness. He therefore shortens his holidays to return to the city which he had left only a few days earlier, "disturbed as though he were being released from prison."[63]

Alexandre Chenevert dominates all characters to such an extent that they attain importance only in relation to him. Rather than being portrayed as distinct personalities, most appear as types, such as the bank manager and the doctor. For this reason only Father Marchand need be singled out. He allows the novelist to further Alexandre Chenevert's questioning regarding the meaning of life and death.

Chenevert's concept of God and his relationship to Him is largely dependent on his perception of his fellowman. As his image of man becomes debased, that of God diminishes to a like degree, just as an ennobling image of man parallels his reconciliation with a majestic God. In the city the tormented man can conceive only of an Old Testament God, a God of wrath and of unbelievable, unspeakable cruelty. In the country, at peace with himself, the bank teller experiences also a hitherto unknown "certainty of God" who reveals himself as a "benign presence."[64] But this image soon changes again as Chenevert reverts to his old misanthropic self.

When the hospital chaplain urges Alexandre Chenevert to prepare himself for his death, Father Marchand, a man of robust health, is gradually forced to recognize his own inadequacy. His wordly experience is far too limited and his own faith has never been tested by suffering. Unlike Chenevert, he has never really been tormented by metaphysical anguish. But he is not a man of simple faith, like the

Capuchin from Toutes-Aides in *La Petite Poule d'Eau,* whose example inspires others and whose love for mankind reaches out to all. Father Marchand is one of those priests "to whom men are endurable only because of God."[65] His message of resignation, the priest must acknowledge, is ineffective against the bank teller's revolt against this apparently meaningless suffering that makes God appear more cruel than any man. But just as his fellowman allows Alexandre Chenevert to attain a nobler perception of both mankind and God, Father Marchand is granted a kind of psychological and spiritual development. It is intimated that with the recognition of the individual's potential greatness, as exemplified by the bank teller, he will no longer be indifferent to the patients to whom he ministers.

As his illness transforms Alexandre Chenevert's vision of man, his vision of God, too, is changed. But as the teller recognizes the compassion that his acquaintances and fellow workers demonstrate in the usual kindnesses extended to a sick man, Alexandre's eyes are suddenly opened to man's greatness. At the same time the greatness of God that he had perceived earlier now seems much inferior to that of mankind. Alexandre Chenevert simply cannot fathom that divine love could equal or be superior to man's example. Just as Chenevert, reconciled with his fellowmen, patterns his vision of God on his positive image of man, he is at last content to imagine paradise in terms of his most idealistic, yet realistic, vision of daily existence on earth. "As Heaven, he could see nothing better than earth, now that men had become good neighbors."[66]

What tragic irony that Alexandre Chenevert—who is indeed Everyman (as well as an individual)—should recognize only at the end of his life that, unknown to him, happiness had always been within his grasp.

Chapter Three
Idyllic Interludes

Gabrielle Roy's consciousness of human misery that is inherent in the human condition, which she expressed so masterfully in *Bonheur d'occasion* and *Alexandre Chenevert,* does not lessen her sensitivity to and appreciation of the beauty of nature and life on a simple level, as illustrated in *La Petite Poule d'Eau* (*Where Nests the Water Hen,* 1950), and *Cet été qui chantait* (*Enchanted Summer,* 1972). But whereas the earlier work exemplifies man's simple life, in harmony with nature; in the later work plants and animals are the major characters and man is only an observer of, rather than a participant in, nature's harmony.

In her review of *Bonheur d'occasion* in the *New York Times* Mary McGrory noted: "American readers, while they must admire the author's vivid characterization, unflinching honesty, and dry-eyed compassion, may find the book heavy-going. They are sure to rebel at its lack of humor."[1] Such reaction to the sombre aspect of Roy's first novel was not unique, as became particularly apparent from the critical reaction to *La Petite Poule d'Eau.* "This book is a sheer delight," Harold C. Gardiner[2] assures his readers. Emphasizing the author's "delightful, fine humor," Gilles Marcotte, for instance, suggests that "rediscovering her country, Gabrielle Roy has apparently found her *joie de vivre* again."[3] Mary McGrory feels that in her second book Gabrielle Roy now "has in contrast to *Bonheur d'occasion* written with a freshness of humor and warmth of understanding that give it [the series of sketches] a pleasant glow."[4] Andrée Maillet holds *La Petite Poule d'Eau* in such high regard that she declares it "above all criticism."[5] William Arthur Deacon, who had earlier spoken so enthusiastically of *Bonheur d'occasion,* is equally magnanimous in his praise of Roy's second book: "No other writer of first rate talents has attempted to recreate for us the life of our remotest frontier. . . . Miss Roy has brought to her unique task a rarely understanding eye, reflected in a style both graceful and gracious."[6] Janet C. Oliver also is particularly appreciative of Roy's style: "Seldom does a story of such beauty of expression and theme appear in print. For this book of Gabrielle Roy's gives one the intellectual and emotional satisfaction of a beautiful poem."[7]

While *Cet été qui chantait (Enchanted Summer)*, too, earned Roy some high praise, particularly by François Ricard[8] and Jean Ethier-Blais,[9] its apparent simplicity and subject matter disconcerted other readers.[10] Some of the criticism directed against this work, which François Ricard regards as "by no means naive" but as Gabrielle Roy's most "utopian projection," may directly depend on today's world atmosphere.[11] On the other hand, some readers may welcome in *Cet été qui chantait*—which Jean Ethier-Blais views as a poem in which nature recorded its history[12]—a world reminiscent of Colette's *Dialogue avec les bêtes (Creatures Great and Small)* or Henri Bosco's *Hyacinthe (The Dark Bough)*.

La Petite Poule d'Eau

The book traces the origin of *La Petite Poule d'Eau (Where Nests the Water Hen)*, a story which the author sees as a study of "humanity without civilization, humanity before civilization" to "an unlikely apposition."[13] Paradoxically, the book that portrays the primitive lives of the islanders of *La Petite Poule d'Eau* was inspired by a visit to one of civilization's greatest achievements, Chartres Cathedral in France. This struck Roy as "the most beautiful jewel man's skill ever created," as she observed in an interview with Ringuet.[14]

As in the case of the two urban novels, *Bonheur d'occasion* and *Alexandre Chenevert*, the Manitoban setting of *La Petite Poule d'Eau*, where the Tousignants live, is described in precise detail. Also, the experiences of the summer of 1937, when Gabrielle Roy taught before leaving for Europe, may well have played a role in shaping the events and characters of that simple, idyllic story. Yet the author's personal contribution is all-important, for, as she declares: "They [the characters] did not exist. I created them." However, "the unconscious is more important in the process of creation than the conscious."[15]

The resulting "dream-like sort of story," Roy sadly admits to Donald Cameron, is one of nostalgia and tragic hope for "it's life as it might have been or could have been, or could be."[16] B. K. Sandwell also affirms its universal meaning: "Simple people doing simple things, but told with such loving care that they become universal, that the Little Water Hen River becomes a symbol of the world."[17]

In stark contrast to *Bonheur d'occasion* and *Alexandre Chenevert*, man is fully attuned to his milieu in *La Petite Poule d'Eau*. The Tousignants' independence amidst their isolation, the reader is given to understand, creates an atmosphere of happiness, peace, and unity. This allows them a sense of freedom to realize their dreams and to plan with confidence for the future. In *Bonheur d'occasion,* on the other hand, the crowded surroundings lead in part to the family's gradual breakup. Luzina Tousignant's destiny—unlike that of Rose-Anna or Florentine—is apparently not tied up with social and political forces beyond her control. The harmonious correspondence between man and nature thus furthers his complete self-realization so that Rose-Anna Lacasse and, to a lesser extent, Alexandre Chenevert may be seen as tragic counterparts to Luzina Tousignant and Father Joseph-Marie.

Luzina Tousignant provides the connecting link for the three parts of *La Petite Poule d'Eau* that are not chronologically arranged and may be read independently. This approach met with mixed critical reactions. Whereas Gordon Roper sees *La Petite Poule d'Eau* as a "novel of selection," akin to Willa Cather's idea of "the novel *démeublé*,"[18] G. A. Vachon, on the other hand, regards these sketches as unsuccessful novels due to the writer's failure to commit herself fully to the fictional universe she sought to create.[19]

"Les Vacances de Luzina" ("Luzina Takes a Holiday"), Part 1, impresses upon the reader from the very beginning the extreme isolation of Little Water Hen Island. The remoteness causes real hazards and imposes hardships on the Tousignants who manage a sheep ranch. But in contrast to *Bonheur d'occasion,* hardships never gain the upper hand. Radiating love for all whose lives she touches, however briefly, Luzina's charisma lies in her ability to reveal to others that they have reasons for happiness. Leaving the island for her "annual vacation," Luzina always returns with the "gift of gifts," another child to whom she has just given birth in the community hospital.

It is not surprising, therefore, that Gabrielle Roy concentrates in her portrait of Luzina Tousignant above all on her role as mother. The author can pay no higher tribute to a woman, for she believes "a successful mother will always be the greatest human accomplishment."[20]

"Serving" her family becomes Luzina's first duty. Her overflowing love and generosity are combined with an exceptional sense of wonder and curiosity. Thus Luzina perceives all human relationships in terms of enrichment. Inevitably captivated by the few works of fiction that reach her, Luzina nevertheless regards her own life as more beautiful and rewarding. Believing that "knowledge . . . confers possession,"[21] she is intent on having her children educated.

Luzina's personal feeling of security undoubtedly allows her to encourage her children's search for independence. Ironically, the schooling, which Luzina attracted to the isolated island for her children's sake, estranges them from their home in later years. As a result of their education, the young people prefer another lifestyle. The separation between the generations manifests itself in *La Petite Poule d'Eau* on the physical and intellectual levels. Luzina's sense of intellectual inferiority is illustrated by her reluctance to address an envelope to her children because it will be scrutinized by strangers. But since they are emotionally secure in their mother's love and pay tribute to her self-sacrifice and dedication, there is no sense of alienation as in *Bonheur d'occasion*.

"L'Ecole de la Petite Poule d'Eau" ("The School on the Little Water Hen"), Part 2, brings the outside world to this idyllic island. Gabrielle Roy relates, frequently with humorous touches, the Tousignants' efforts to get a school for their children and the comings and goings of the various teachers.

Without permanent teachers the children's formal education is naturally inconsistent and incomplete. But, what is more important, Roy suggests, the teachers' different personalities and approaches to education encourage tolerance in the children.

Mademoiselle Côté's youth and love for children attract the shy, loving Tousignant children almost instantly. The desire to please their charming mistress encourages them to learn. Geography lessons and pride in their French heritage are among the most vivid memories associated with the island's first teachers.

Miss O'Rorke, on the other hand, an eccentric old maid who forever finds fault with her surroundings, is a rigid disciplinarian from whom the children learn rather reluctantly. The opportunistic Luzina must impress upon them therefore that the teacher's lack of French gives them an ideal opportunity to learn English. Whereas Luzina always succeeds in seeing others to their advantage, the eccentric English lady recognizes only upon leaving the benefits of her position.

Perhaps the best teacher of all is Armand Dubreuil. Yet he is least interested in teaching, or at least in formal instruction. Proclaiming "nature as his system," he prefers hunting and even leaves the island early. Also, since he greatly appreciates the paradisaic atmosphere of the area, he advises Luzina to close her school lest "discontent, . . . the root of all progress"[22] destroy their peaceful existence.

In addition to the physical and emotional-intellectual aspects highlighted in Parts 1 and 2 respectively, as Annette Saint-Pierre has pointed out,[23] Gabrielle Roy expands her vision in Part 3, "Le Capuchin de Toutes-Aides" ("The Capuchin from Toutes-Aides"), to the role of religion in the lives of the Tousignants.

Father Joseph-Marie is a man of simple faith whose understanding of human nature and capacity for love is somewhat like Luzina's, although her sphere of influence is, of course, more limited. "The world's pain remained inviolate for him, always inexplicable; but the same held true for joy and love."[24] The good-hearted man inspires Luzina at once with awe and gratitude for "God's annual visit" and motherly devotion for his daily needs. A man of action, the Capuchin is intent on answering his parishioners' earthly and spiritual needs. Being "free to love," he spreads a message of freedom and love among his flock from many nations in his widespread "parish" in plain words and with illustrations from their daily lives.

The geographical confines of *La Petite Poule d'Eau* are narrow indeed. But Gabrielle Roy peoples the area with many nationalities that realistically conform to the Canadian "mosaic." The people whom Luzina meets on her annual outings include the Jew Abe Zlutkin who always speaks with pride of his wife. The Bjorgssons, an Icelandic family, for one night offer Luzina the hospitality of their home. In town she meets Anton Gusaliek, the Ukrainian, Mrs. McFarlane and Aggie from Scotland, as well as Nick Sluzick's family. And the Mackenzies, the Tousignants' closest neighbors, are Metis Indians. In the contacts of such diverse nationalities, language frequently presents a barrier. But this occurs only on a superficial level, the author suggests, if the individual lets his heart speak. And as Luzina's example illustrates how barriers may be overcome on a personal level, Father Joseph-Marie also draws people to himself from other religions, Jews and Protestants, to support his cause.

Cet été qui chantait

Cet été qui chantait (*Enchanted Summer,* 1972) recalls the colors/ sights, fragrances, and sounds (emphasized in the French title mean-

ing "The Summer That Sang") in Charlesvoix in northern Quebec where Gabrielle Roy, "a sensitive painter of nature,"[25] as Paula G. Lewis observes, regularly spends the summer months.

One selection, "L'Enfant morte" ("The Dead Child"), however, creates a link with Manitoba. Also in this later work the sense of feeling and atmosphere has become even more important than in the earlier *La Petite Poule d'Eau*. At the same time the mood is more sombre, or at least more subdued. The humor that was an important element in avoiding sentimentality and melodrama in *La Petite Poule d'Eau* now is almost totally absent. *Cet été qui chantait* which "captures in luminous prose what is most poetic in country living"[26] is a celebration of life where animals and plants—a bullfrog, crows, cows, daisies, and trees, among others—are personified. Indeed, of the nineteen brief sketches only two have human characters as central figures. Nature's cycle instills in man both a sense of his mortality and of his fundamental solitude. Man's communication with nature then is perhaps encouraged by his instinctive need to overcome that solitude. Inasmuch as animal and plant life presents again and again a mirror of human existence, man is brought closer to nature. Although these reminiscences, frequently with religious overtones, do not serve as parables, the animals and plant life displayed before the author's eyes and shared with the reader are seen as a microcosm of our universe. Again and again the writer draws explicit parallels or intersperses these anecdotes with philosophical comments. Thus in "La Gatte de monsieur Emile" ("Monsieur Emile's Gatte") with its description of the transformation of the "gatte"—an apparently lifeless piece of earth into a richly flowering area—she notes, "But plants are like people. The moment a group is happily settled somewhere, everyone wants to move in."[27] Or in "La Nuit des lucioles" (The Night of the Fireflies") Gabrielle Roy muses: "Perhaps fireflies live only long enough to give forth their fleeing light. Like all of us. Fortunate are those who at least once before they are extinguished shine with their full light. Caught in God's fire."[28]

The relation between man and nature may be even more intimate, so that animals become observers of the people around them, have a degree of intelligence, and act much like human beings. Thus the sketch entitled "Les Vaches d'Aimé" ("Aimé's Cows") presents a brief reflection of the neighbor's cows' reaction to the city lady's (the author's) visit. In "La Messe aux hirondelles" ("The Mass of the Swallows")—which a delighted Paul Gay regards as "pure Daudet"[29]—the animals appear to participate in the celebration of mass, or, as Roy and her friend lament the absence of the bullfrog's sounds in "De retour à la mare de monsieur Toong" ("Once More to the Pool of Monsieur Toong"), "the birds were reproaching us for our paltry human questions. 'All are not happy at the same moment,' they reminded us."[30]

Such attempts to reconcile nature and mankind, to expose the inner world of the outer reality at hand, conform to Gabrielle Roy's tendency to look beyond appearances. But a thin line separates these reflections from oversentimentality and melodrama, and, as François Ricard points out, the reader must not judge *Cet été qui chantait* as "realistic," but must rather align himself with Roy on the "imaginary" or "mythical" levels in her "dream of innocence."[31]

As François Hébert suggests, weakness lies in Gabrielle Roy's attempt to be too explicit at times and the animals' words are superfluous.[32] For the reader who is willing to suspend his critical judgment, however, and who can accept the magic of Roy's work, it will be an "Enchanted Summer," as the English title indicates. This requires also a childlike reader, and it is noteworthy that Roy dedicates this work "to the children of all seasons with the wish that they will never tire of listening to their planet Earth."[33]

While this "Ode to Joy"[34] concentrates on re-creating the moods and rhythms of one summer, the author's reflections are at once timeless and of significance for the future and draw, consciously and unconsciously, on the experiences and wisdom of the past. Thus the celebration of life cannot deny the precariousness of life, and memories of death or the anticipation of death are both prominent. This is evident in "L'Enfant morte" ("The Dead Child") and "Le Jour où Martine descendit au fleuve" ("The Day Martine Went Down to the River"). But though death, or at least man's consciousness of his mortality, may be ever-present, in contrast to the horrors of dying and death presented in *Alexandre Chenevert,* death is seen here essentially as an integral part of life.

In "L'Enfant morte" Gabrielle Roy wonders why sad reflections should suddenly and inexplicably intrude on "the summer that sang." And she relives her first day as a teacher in a very poor village. Hurt by the children's "inconceivable distance," she successfully breaks down their barriers when she suggests they all visit a schoolmate who had died the evening before.

In "Le Jour où Martine descendit au fleuve" Roy recalls the old woman's yearning "to see the river once again before she died."[35] Restless, Cousin Martine, "a soul straining towards God,"[36] recollects along the familiar shores her whole life and asks herself once again about the meaning of life: "She was content at last that she had lived."[37] Her homecoming to the river is a kind of pilgrimage that brings to mind Christine's mother whose return to the hills of Altamont is related in the title section of *La Route d'Altamont*. Both in this latter work and in *Rue Deschambault* communion with the self and the search for the meaning of life will be given more direct and extensive treatment.

Two Children's Stories

Ma Vache Bossie ("My Cow Bossie," 1976) and *Courte-Queue* (*Cliptail*, 1979) deserve to be discussed briefly. Young readers may well recall in later years these two children's stories as an introduction to the works of Gabrielle Roy. They will then note that these two books are linked, despite their differences, to the mainstream of Roy's work.

Whereas *Courte-Queue* is characterized by a poetic mode, *Ma Vache Bossie* is indicative of the author's more direct and realistic style. *Ma Vache Bossie* was originally published in 1963 with minor variations in a rural magazine. The events that led to the account of this tale might well have happened on Rue Deschambault, and the first-person narrator does bear a resemblance to Christine. But it is fortunate that *Ma Vache Bossie* is not included in *Rue Deschambault* or *La Route d'Altamont,* for Gabrielle Roy's approach in *Ma Vache Bossie* is closer to the style of her journalistic writings than the two more personal volumes evoking her childhood reminiscences.

In contrast, the tone and atmosphere of *Courte-Queue* are such that this story might well have been incorporated in *Cet été qui chantait*. While this tale of a whimsical cat justly earned for its author the Canada Council's prize for the best children's story in French in 1979, adult readers are certainly more appreciative of the poetic use of language.

The gift of a cow to the eight-year-old narrator who remains anonymous is the basis for the amusing anecdote recounted in *Ma Vache Bossie*. The well-intentioned birthday gift brings with it unsuspected problems for the young owner whose family is totally unprepared and unsuited to care for the animal.

Bossie is resold after a year. While the child's business skills have improved during that period, she discovers to her dismay that the apparent profit derived from the sale of the cow's milk had already been spent on hay, and she must repay her mother for the expenses that she had considered a loan. The humorous touches in Roy's telling save this tale from the somber associations that characterize *Bonheur d'occasion* or "Le Déménagement" ("The Move") in *La Route d'Altamont,* for example.

The name of Courte-Queue, that provided the title for Gabrielle Roy's second children's story, is a permanent reminder of one of the cat's first misadventures. When she was still a kitten, the farm dog bit off part of her tail.

Later, when the cat's first litter is drowned, Courte-Queue adopts other kittens. To save these little ones, she takes them to mysterious hiding places. As winter approaches, however, she must put her trust in her mistress Berthe—whom readers first met in *Cet été qui chantait*—for the sake of her charges. The author relates with great warmth the changing relationship between the cat and her mistress, as the animal's trust convinces Berthe against all reason to keep yet another lot of unwanted kittens on the farm.

Louise Pomminville's bold and bright illustrations and François Olivier's delicate and more subdued drawings for *Ma Vache Bossie* and *Courte-Queue,* respectively, reflect the varied styles of these two works admirably.

Chapter Four
A Pilgrimage to the Past

Rue Deschambault and *La Route d'Altamont*

By virtue of its very title, *Rue Deschambault* (*Street of Riches*, 1957) draws attention to the intensely personal nature of this series of childhood sketches as it recalls Gabrielle Roy's birthplace and childhood home. On the one hand, we note the usual prefatory comment: "Certain events in this narrative took place in real life; but the characters and almost everything that happens to them are products of the imagination."[1] On the other hand, the author readily acknowledges the work's autobiographical background: "Much of it does indeed run parallel to my own life. The setting and atmosphere are those of Saint-Boniface where I grew up. But, naturally, I have transposed my remembrances—already transformed by the passing of years—and perhaps—I hope I have succeeded—transfigured them."[2] These observations bring to mind Colette's reflections in *Break of Day:* "Is anyone imagining as he reads me, that I'm portraying myself? Have patience: this is merely my model."[3]

In "transfiguring" her experiences, Gabrielle Roy is so successful that *Street of Riches,* the English title of *Rue Deschambault,* is most appropriate. The blending of autobiography and fiction, that is comparable to the style of Colette that Roy admired, also characterizes the sequel to *Rue Deschambault, La Route d'Altamont* (*The Road Past Altamont,* 1966), "a book" which Robert Cormier "finds touched with tender magic."[4]

Choosing Christine as the narrator of the eighteen vignettes collected in *Rue Deschambault* and of the four short stories assembled in *La Route d'Altamont,* Gabrielle Roy portrays a series of characters and relates incidents that touched her life from preschool days in "Les Deux Nègres" ("The Two Negroes") to adolescence in "Gagner ma vie" ("To Earn My Living") in *Rue Deschambault.* Taking up her self-quest again in *La Route d'Altamont,* she returns to early childhood

with "Ma grand-mère toute-puissante" ("My Almighty Grandmother") and concludes it with the title story of "La Route
d'Altamont," recalling events of early adulthood. *La Route d'Altamont*
is again an opportune choice as title for, as will be seen later on, the
excursion that takes Christine and her mother on "the road past Altamont" in southern Manitoba comes to symbolize for the young
woman both an ending and a beginning, the crossroads between her
life at home and an independent future.

The publication of *Rue Deschambault* was greeted, with few excep-
tions, with generous praise, as exemplified by the critiques by Pierre
Lagarde,[5] Pierre de Grandpré,[6] and Andrée Maillet.[7] The three following opinions are indicative of the general tenor.

Guy Robert saw in *Rue Deschambault* "one of the most original and
most successful works"[8] in French-Canadian literature. "Miss Roy has
seen and felt an innate sadness of life and learned to communicate it
beautifully. It emerges, this subdued feeling, with a beauty which is
quite indescribable in the logical terms of critical prose. Miss Roy
comes very close to the writing of poetry that is soft-voiced tragedy,"
remarks Ted Honderich.[9] While in the words of Miriam Waddington, Roy "has attained the point of development where her style is
nothing more or less than her individuality. And it is this individuality, this Gabrielle Roy-ness, which comes through on these pages
as naturally, as intimately, and as inevitably as the life process
itself."[10]

La Route d'Altamont was acclaimed even more fervently. Gilles Marcotte[11] emphasized that this book of childhood reminiscences could
have been written only by a most mature writer. A similar opinion
leads David Helwig to remark that *La Route d'Altamont* is "a work of
meaning and wisdom."[12] At the same time Roy leads her readers into
"an enchanted kingdom," notes André Major[13] with delight. Josephine Braden also finds *La Route d'Altamont* an "unusual, enchanting
book." Recalling Katherine Mansfield's childhood sketches, this
American critic concludes: "Faultless writers both, both sure of their
impressions and able to work them so that the reader is truly
touched, not just reached."[14]

Before analyzing in greater depth Gabrielle Roy's technique and
the contents of *Rue Deschambault* and *La Route d'Altamont* let us briefly
identify the particular experiences that inspired the author to share
her memories with her readers. In Roy's life this period ranges, as

François Ricard notes, approximately from 1911 to 1928 and from 1911 to 1937 in *Rue Deschambault* and *La Route d'Altamont* respectively.[15]

In *Rue Deschambault* "Petite Misère" ("Petite Misère") refers to little Christine herself and throws light on her father's tragic character. "Les Déserteuses" ("The Gadabouts") provides a vivid portrait of Christine's vivacious mother. Her joy in living and yearning for freedom are such that "perhaps to be a better wife," she visits Quebec with her youngest child without informing her husband whose work frequently takes him away from home for long periods. The father's contrasting somber character is highlighted in "Le Puits de Dunrea" ("The Well of Dunrea"), recalling a disastrous fire. The parents' opposing natures are symbolically epitomized for the adolescent Christine in the selection entitled "Le Jour et la nuit" ("By Day and By Night").

"Pour empêcher un mariage" ("To Prevent a Marriage"), "Un bout de ruban jaune" ("A Bit of Yellow Ribbon"), and "Alicia" ("Alicia"), which focus on three of Christine's older sisters, emphasize the strange ambivalence that exists at times between the world of adults and that of a child.

Among the members of Christine's expanding family circle, "Ma tante Thérésina Veilleux" ("My Aunt Theresina Veilleux") evokes particularly vivid memories. "Les deux nègres" ("The Two Negroes"), "L'Italienne" ("L'Italienne" [*sic*]), and "Wilhelm" ("Wilhelm") remind Christine of some of her family's earliest contacts with various members of Canada's diversified ethnic population. While the mature Christine looks back on her experiences with some humor, Gabrielle Roy forcefully illustrates in these selections how the serenity of a child's and an adolescent's universe may be threatened by adult prejudices. Accounts of the loss the "Le Titanic" ("The *Titanic*") also brought to the attention of the ever-inquisitive Christine a fascinating, yet somewhat frightening world since it raised questions about God's hand in men's lives. "A major excellence of this book," as Samuel J. Hazo emphasizes, "is that Miss Roy's occasional concern with misfortune . . . does not sour her portrayal of incidents of human joy."[16]

Memories of "Mon chapeau rose" ("My Pink Hat"), "Les Bijoux" ("The Jewels"), and "La Tempête" ("The Storm") allow Christine to laugh at herself as she recalls some of her most carefree and vain moments. "Ma coqueluche" ("My Whooping Cough"), "La Voix des étangs" ("The Voice of the Pools"), and "Gagner ma vie . . ." ("To Earn My Living"), on the other hand, are of particular interest as they illumine the root of Christine's nascent artistic vocation.

In her endeavor to gain increasing self-knowledge, Gabrielle Roy, transposed as Christine, re-creates once again in *La Route d'Altamont* the scenes and characters of her earlier years. Thus in "Ma Grand-mère toute-puissante" ("My Almighty Grandmother"), the first of the four selections, Christine pays tribute to the creative gifts of the old woman who made a doll for her six-year-old grandchild. As she looks back on herself in "Le Vieillard et l'enfant" ("The Old Man and the Child"), she remembers the intimate relationship that enriched both parties, however disparate it may have seemed to others.

One of the bitterest disappointments of Christine's childhood is associated with "Le Déménagement" ("The Move"). On this occasion the eleven-year-old's adventurous spirit is tested by an unexpectedly cruel aspect of reality as she observes the moving of a poor family, who, like the Lacasses of *Bonheur d'occasion,* are forced to move to an even poorer area. The final selection, "La Route d'Altamont" ("The Road Past Altamont"), then focuses on a Christine who is more mature than the one who spoke of "Gagner ma vie . . ." ("To Earn My Living") at the end of *Rue Deschambault.* Equally decisive in Roy's life is the decision to go beyond "La Route d'Altamont" and to turn to Europe "to learn to know myself."[17]

In the final analysis, however, as Elizabeth L. Dalton judiciously affirms: "It is not the action in the four episodes [of *La Route d'Altamont*], that makes for beauty. Rather it is the open window into human hearts that causes the reader to reflect upon changing relationships and the universal seeking for something just beyond."[18]

The return to the past thus enriches both the author and the reader. Gabrielle Roy's "remembrances of things past" frequently extend beyond the purely personal experiences to profound insights as these experiences are viewed and described in terms of childhood, yet filtered and enlightened by the mature writer's understanding. This brings to mind Proust's reflections: " 'My readers' . . . they would not be my readers but readers of themselves, my book serving merely as a sort of magnifying glass. . . . Consequently I would not ask them to praise or dispraise me but only to tell me if it is as I say, if the words they read in themselves are, indeed, the same as I have written."[19]

Significance of Childhood and
Narrative Technique

The publication of *La Route d'Altamont* almost ten years after *Rue Deschambault* also suggests that Gabrielle Roy, who began her series of childhood vignettes in her middle forties, would subscribe to François Mauriac's belief that "Childhood is all-important for it provides the key to life."[20]

In both *Rue Deschambault* and *La Route d'Altamont*, Roy's readers are immersed in a world of enchantment, whose style and atmosphere are reminiscent of the autobiographical works of such writers as Colette, Marcel Pagnol, or Henri Bosco. At the same time it must be acknowledged that such "transfigurations" do not always respond to the temperament of readers who prefer such a work as Simone de Beauvoir's *Mémoires d'une jeune fille rangée (Memoirs of a Dutiful Daughter)*.

The importance Roy attaches to childhood and her continuous exploration of it as a creative writer may well be epitomized by Christine's suggestion that life is "to find one's childhood again."[21] It is a vital experience for, as the French poet and critic Franz Hellens notes, "Childhood is not something that dies within us. . . . It is not a memory . . . it continues to enrich us unknown to us."[22]

The significance of memory in Roy's work brings to mind Willa Cather's apparently paradoxical observation: "Life began for me when I ceased to admire and began to remember."[23] The rediscovery of the past, therefore, does not represent escapism. Instead it becomes essential for a better understanding of the present and an appreciation of the "successive beings it [life] makes of us as we increase in age,"[24] as Roy terms it. "Without the past, what are we? . . . Severed plants, half alive!"[25] Christine's mother muses.

Gabrielle Roy's sincerity in no small measure contributes to the authentic vision of childhood and youth in *Rue Deschambault* and *La Route d'Altamont*. Memories do not, of course, conform to a rational order. Yet in their artistic re-creation or representation a certain order or rhythm becomes necessary. Just as the author of fiction creates order out of chaos, Christine (the fictionalized Gabrielle Roy) seeks to establish the meaning and order of her life. Indeed, *Rue Deschambault* and *La Route d'Altamont* support Hans Meyerhoff's conclusion: "Creative imagination is creative recall. . . . To construct a work of art is to reconstruct the world of experience and the self. And thus a concept of the self emerges, through the act of creative recall translated into a process of artistic creation, displaying characteristics of unity and continuity which would not be attributed to the self as given in immediate experience."[26] Both voluntary and involuntary memory, as Henri Bergson termed it, may serve as a catalyst. This is illustrated in "Ma tante Thérésina Veilleux" and La Voix des étangs" respectively, both in *Rue Deschambault*. Thus, although the individual selections of the two collections are apparently rearranged in chronological order, Gabrielle Roy does not falsify her impressions in an attempt to re-create a uniform and complete picture. Also, as she draws to the reader's attention, occasionally even large segments of time seem to be lost or long periods seem condensed. This is seen, for example, in "Ma coqueluche" in *Rue Deschambault*, where she recalls that a gift of chimes transformed that whole summer, when she was recuperating in her hammock, into a single moment of quiet joy.

The first-person narrative predominates in the quest of the self, and Roy's fictional counterpart is the central figure in six sketches in *Rue Deschambault* and in all four selections in *La Route d'Altamont*. However, as Christine's focus shifts from herself to that of various family members, relatives, and others whose lives touch hers as her world expands, the narrator's personal perspective is complemented by the observation of other participants. Thus "memories" of persons or events are introduced to which the little Christine could not have been a party. A striking example is "Le Puits de Dunrea." Here it falls on the older Agnes to reveal to the rest of the family an aspect of their father's personality generally kept hidden.

It is also noteworthy that as the more mature Roy probes more deeply into her past, the creative writer feels the need for more developed sketches than those in *Rue Deschambault*. The two volumes are therefore essentially of equal length. In both works the time intervals vary greatly between the individual incidents Christine relates. Also, in *Rue Deschambault* in particular, there are few precise references to Christine's age.

Essentially time is conceived as a cycle, so that the future contains the past while the past anticipates the future. Both retrospective and prospective views are present. The artist re-creates the past as the child Christine experiences (rather than experienced) it in its original immediacy and depth. At the same time the mature Christine focuses on the present and the transformation that has occurred in her, as the factual accounts of the past are complemented by reflections of the present moment. This is evident, for example, in "Petite Misère"

("Petite Misère" [*sic*]) in which Christine recalls one of the most painful memories associated with her strange nickname—"Little Miss Misery"—when she was probably about six years old: "But one day he [father] hurled the hateful name at me in anger. I don't even know any longer what can have deserved such an explosion; probably some mere trifle; my father went through long periods of dark moodiness. . . . Later on I understood that, constantly fearing for us both the least and the worst of evils, he especially wanted to put us early on guard against too great a yearning for happiness."[27] In clearly distinguishing the adult's perceptions from the child's, Roy masters one of the most difficult problems for writers dealing with childhood.

Even as a child, however, Roy suggests, Christine was conscious of a dual role. "I had a tendency to divide into two people, actor and witness,"[28] she recalls, as she pictures herself once again on the horse-drawn cart in "Le Déménagement."

Christine's Return to *Rue Deschambault* and *La Route d'Altamont*

Gabrielle Roy's aspirations to rediscover the feeling of exaltation and magic of her childhood and her endeavor to communicate this to her readers succeeded eminently. But it would be erroneous to assume that *Rue Deschambault* presents this view of childhood as a paradise, as will become apparent upon closer examination of some of the individual selections.

While each reader may well have personal preferences for a given sketch in *Rue Deschambault* and *La Route d'Altamont,* is not "Petite Misère" for all of us one of the most poignant and unforgettable selections of these collections? "Petite Misère"—a term both of endearment and frustration—culminates in little Christine's utter despair and sense of desolation when her father, in a moment of forgetfulness and despondency, deplores the fact that he ever had children. The child's memories are complemented by the adult's superior understanding and interpretation of the event: "Parents think that such words, well beyond the understanding of children, do them no harm; but precisely because they are only half intelligible to them, children ponder them and make of them a torture."[29]

The nickname "Petite Misère" epitomizes both the older man's frustrations with himself and his love for his favorite. The tortured man fears for his youngest, whose sensitivity to the world's suffering so greatly resembles his own. The recognition of this common trait, however, threatens to create a barrier between the two, as Christine instinctively seeks to repress that aspect of her nature, sensing how great her father's unspoken suffering is. The poignancy of the child's almost unbearable and unspeakable pain that day will never be forgotten. Yet that incident is transmuted into an experience of love. How true it is that the manner shows the intent. That evening Christine's father once again calls out: "Little One! Petite Misère!" And the little girl, who had retreated to the attic, responds to her father's love that he sought to express in baking for her a "leaden" rhubarb pie which the two "valiantly strove to swallow."[30]

While "Petite Misère" is rooted in Gabrielle Roy's personal experience, "Alicia"—which Samuel J. Hazo[31] regards as equal to the best pages of Willa Cather—is one of the most moving "products of the imagination."[32] Ironically, Christine's sister, whose mental illness is induced in part by her oversensitivity to the suffering of others, herself causes unfathomable anguish to her family. The well-intentioned parents' attempt to shelter Christine from the truth, however, only increases the child's apprehensions. She asks herself: "Is this what constitutes childhood: by means of lies, to be kept in worlds apart?"[33]

Her parents' disparate natures puzzle and even disconcert the young Christine for they seem to challenge her sense of loyalty. "Le Puits de Dunrea" and "Les Déserteuses" concentrate respectively on illustrating the father's melancholy and the mother's joyful nature.

Ever since calamity struck the village of Dunrea, as we learn from "Le Puits de Dunrea," Christine's father has been burdened by a strange sense of guilt. Recognizing that he had always loved the Dukhobors better than any of the other immigrants under his care, he was especially proud of their achievements. When fire struck the community during one of his visits, he interpreted this disaster as a form of divine punishment for his pride. As he communicates his fear of God's wrath to the distraught settlers, he unwittingly endangers their lives, for instead of fleeing the settlement, they return to the burning church in the desperate hope that their prayers may pacify the Lord. Later, when Christine's father found refuge in the village well, the distraught man believed himself already dead. Only a vision of his daughter Agnes awaiting his return rekindled his will to live. But the feeling that he had "judged God" remained an intolerable burden to him.

The amusing account of a surreptitious trip to Quebec in "Les

Déserteuses" throws light on Christine's ambiguous feelings toward her parents. It elucidates at the same time the child's changing perception of her parents' true love for each other.

Her mother's inclination toward freedom arouses the jealousy in her youngest, still a preschooler. She is somewhat reassured only when her mother's traveling plans include her. Insofar as her mother's aspirations and "traveling madness"[34] are in conflict with a woman's traditional role, the parents' dream basically seems forever irreconcilable, as the adult Christine recognizes in later life. Neither parent understood that each of them sought, needed even, what was denied to them in their daily lives. Thus Papa, whose occupation requires a "wandering life,"[35] expects at home tranquillity and permanence. Then, too, neither of the parents apparently realized that they could have experienced so much more happiness if they had been able to express their true feelings for each other more freely, as they were wont to do in the company of strangers.

However fascinated Christine may be by Canada's vastness and beauty, the little girl is also an astute observer of her mother and the rejuvenating effect their trip has on her. She feels therefore somewhat resentful toward Papa, holding him responsible for her mother's usual lack of youthfulness.

Her mother's image of her father, too, no longer conforms to her own: "throughout our journey Maman had been discovering so many fine traits in Papa, I somehow felt I no longer knew him very well."[36] As they approach home, Maman again undergoes a change. She seems suddenly aged and worried, reproaching herself for abandoning her loved ones. And yet, as she tries to explain to a fellow traveler, she left "perhaps to become a better wife."[37] Intuitively the precocious child understands where the adult's logic fails. "It is when you leave your own that you truly find them, and you are happy about it; you wish them well; and you want also to be better yourself."[38]

A similarly revealing portrait of Christine's parents is sketched in "Le Jour et la nuit" whose title epitomizes for Christine their opposing natures. For the adolescent Christine it is not always easy to reconcile within herself her inherited traits. "Morning seemed to me the time of logic, night of something perhaps truer than logic. . . . I was divided between these two sides of my nature, which came to me from my parents, sundered by the day and the night."[39] Self-indulgence is a luxury the mature Christine denies herself. As she looks back on the past, she regrets the egotism of her youth. She attributes her incomplete knowledge of her father to sins of omission.

Responding to critics' claims, already mentioned, that Roy's male characters are weakly drawn, Adrien Thério finds that the portrait of Edouard is at least equal, if not superior, to that of his wife.[40]

Rue Deschambault, however, is not without humor, and Christine does not shy away from revealing her foibles. In "Mon chapeau rose" is a reminder of the little girl's vanity and at times too-adventurous spirit. Similarly, in "Les Bijoux" Christine smiles at her former fickleness as she recalls her adolescent infatuation with cheap jewelry and perfumes and going from one extreme to the other—nursing lepers in Africa.

The adult Christine can smile at herself also with indulgence when she recalls her first love. This experience, recorded in "Wilhelm," has left her with bittersweet memories. Fearing that the adolescent's infatuation with the "Hollander" could lead to a permanent relationship, the well-meaning parents destroyed with their ridicule of the "foreigner" something of the young girl's intuitive acceptance of others for their own sake without regard for differences in nationality. The disconcerting duality of adult values is strikingly illustrated when Wilhelm, having returned to his homeland, no longer presents a threat in the parents' minds and is suddenly a most desirable and virtuous young man.

Christine's future vocation or profession receives extensive treatment in *Rue Deschambault* and *La Route d'Altamont.* In this regard "Ma coqueluche," "La Voix des étangs," and "Gagner ma vie . . . ," as well as "Ma Grand-mère toute-puissante" and La Route d'Altamont" all mark significant steps in Christine's growth to maturity. These selections, written over a period of about ten years, also provide important insight into Gabrielle Roy's conception of the creative process and on a broader scale the artist's self-concept and his role in society.

The growing self-awareness and search for identity presented the adolescent Christine with some problems so that, as she recalls in "Les Bijoux," "to be oneself is precisely the hardest of all."

The summer of "Ma coqueluche" is therefore recalled with special fondness. That year, when she must have been about eight years old, the child convalescing from whooping cough was in complete harmony with herself as she spent hours in her hammock listening to the ceaseless music of a simple glass chime.

"Ma coqueluche" is an outstanding illustration of how time apparently "lost" may be recovered through art. If memory is to re-create the past in its original intensity, such "lost time" may even be vital for the budding artist. The time of apparent repose spent dreaming seems necessary to allow for absorption and internalization of material upon which the artist may draw later.

In speaking of Christine's aspiration as a writer, Roy attributes much of herself to the character she creates or "re-creates." It is an ideal illustration of Louis Dudek's observation that on the one hand: "The 'I' in literature is as much a creation of the writer's imagination as any of the characters in the novel." On the other hand, "a playwright or novelist can give life to certain characters and not to others. He can only bring to life in another form what is already alive in some form within himself."[41]

The idea of her future occupation presented itself mysteriously, yet irrevocably to the adolescent Christine one spring while listening to the song of the frogs, as she recalls in "La Voix des étangs." When Christine confides in her mother, she discovers that the question she has been asking herself and her doubts are only too justified. But she perceives also the older woman's deep understanding of the creative process. While Christine is indeed sensitive to the hardships an artist faces, her youthful spirit refuses to reconcile itself to the necessity of his solitude.

In attributing to the adolescent Christine the decision to become a writer, the author of *Rue Deschambault* departs from the facts of her own life. As we know, Roy began writing in France in her early thirties. In the presentation of the role of the writer and the goal of the artist, that is, the essential rather than the particular, however, Roy's ideas conform with those of Christine.

The necessity of "earning a living" is most disconcerting to the idealistic Christine, for it presents a bitter clash between reality and the world of her imagination. Again drawing on her personal experiences, Roy portrays how Christine, constrained by monetary needs, and also reluctant to oppose her mother's hopes—like Gabrielle Roy—agrees to become a teacher.

For Christine, as for her creator, teaching in a little prairie village would prove to be a most rewarding experience. The children respond with genuine warmth and instinctive trust to the young teacher whose faith in youth and confidence in the future are thereby strengthened. Thus *Rue Deschambault* concludes on an idealistic note that corresponds to the author's personal philosophy.

For Christine such harmony with herself and her milieu, however, can only be temporary. As we learn from "La Route d'Altamont," the "summons" to become a writer is directly linked with the yearning, even need, to discover the world and must be obeyed despite the hardships it imposes on her and her mother.

For Christine the pursuit of the unknown is essential before she can return to the known and give expression to the world around her. She cannot yet fully accept the wisdom of her mother's conviction: "A writer really needs nothing but a quiet room, some paper, and himself. . . ."[42] Much like her mother, who once left her husband to become a better wife, the aspiring writer feels she must temporarily leave home to find her true identity.

Once again Gabrielle Roy reveals in this short story her ambivalent feelings about leaving home and questions more extensively an artist's struggle with the self and his role in society. Thus Christine's portrait complements on a more personal level that of Pierre Cadorai in *La Montagne secrète* (*The Hidden Mountain,* 1961), as will be seen in chapter 5.

The paradox between the artist's solidarity with men and the solitude of a privileged, godlike being which Gabrielle Roy has illustrated in her fictional works and which springs from her own beliefs and personal struggle extends also to the concept of the creative act as being unique, yet capable of manifesting itself at the same time in every human being in some of the humblest acts. This is made particularly explicit in her essay "Terre des Hommes" ("Man and His World," 1967). The roots of this philosophy, however, go back to the author's childhood experiences that found expression in "Ma Grand-mère toute-puissante."

For Christine the simplicity and wonder of creation are indelibly associated with an event that occurred when she was six years old, when her grandmother made a doll for her. As the child watches the creative process, she is also initiated into the mystery of creation. For however small its beginnings may be, at their best, man's creative endeavors manifest a spark of divinity. The child's intuitive perception of this culminates in her declaration: "You're like God, . . . You're just like God. You can make things out of nothing as He does."[43]

Burdened by a sense of uselessness in her old age, Grandmother is naturally pleased by the child's tribute. At the same time she is humble and points out to the little girl her limitations. For Christine, however, Grandmother remains "Almighty," and her image of the old woman is intimately linked with her vision of God.

Gabrielle Roy's belief in the fundamental nobility of man—as expounded in "Terre des Hommes"—explains her confidence that we all share in the "creative" process that manifests itself in such diversity. Once again, however, as in so many other instances, Roy also presents the other side of the coin. Christine, who had exulted in her grandmother's greatness, a year or so later is puzzled as she witnesses the old woman's increasing feebleness that renders her a shadow of her former self.

"Ma Grand-mère toute-puissante" concludes with the image of little Christine showing her paralyzed grandmother her photograph album. The child gains thereby a vague understanding of the changes that time effects in all of us and of the cyclical nature of life, "catching up with one another,"[44] as Gabrielle Roy calls it.

"Catching up with one another," a major theme of the titular story of *La Route d'Altamont,* directly links the first and last selections of this volume. Roy comments on its meaning in these terms: " 'The Road Past Altamont' is the meeting of people after the present. It's a sort of narrowed circle, where you understand your mother when you reach the age when she said such a thing and you were not able to understand. It's a tragedy, and it's also a very beautiful thing, because eventually you get there."[45]

The immediate impetus to these reflections is the account of two excursions—or their remembrance—by Christine and her mother. For Christine, now a young woman eager to go to Europe, happiness and the future present themselves like the vast expanse of the prairie of which she is a true child. The mother, on the other hand, must turn to the past for her rewards.

Yearning for the landscape of her Quebec childhood, Christine's mother is overjoyed at the unexpected sight of the Pembina Hills on the Altamont road that, as Gérard Bessette has noted, have an effect comparable to Proust's "madeleine."[46] A mysterious communion seems to unite the hills of the old and present times and the adventurous woman who apparently explores the past rather than the future, for life now presents itself to her as a cycle rather than a road ahead of her.

Much as Christine had been her father's confidante, as recalled in "Le Jour et la nuit," the young woman now is her mother's. The interrelation between two generations, first introduced in "Petite Misère," assumes increasing importance as Christine approaches adulthood. Like a leitmotif it recurs again and again in *Rue Deschambault* and *La Route d'Altamont,* especially with regard to the mother-daughter relationship. Occasionally the idea of "My Mother/My Self"[47] suggests an unwelcome bondage, as seen in *Bonheur d'occasion.* In its essence, however, it is positive. That this should be so is hardly surprising in light of Gabrielle Roy's admiration for her mother.

The themes of the child as the essential image of human continuity and the cyclical movements of life that are so vividly illustrated in "La Route d'Altamont" and "Ma Grand-mère toute-puissante" also figure prominently in "Le Vieillard et l'enfant." This story is a tribute to a friendship that unites the young and the old because fundamentally: "Perhaps everything finally forms a circle . . . the end and the beginning had their own way of finding each other."[48] The child's probing questions regarding love, beginning and end, youth and aging, life and death and eternity, frequently touch the very essence of this wise gentleman.

This leads to a dialogue calling forth more and more questions, like ripples of a stone hitting water, but whose meaning, the child knows, escapes her because of its very depth. Since life and death are ultimately inseparable, Gabrielle Roy reminds us, any celebration of individual growth is also a celebration of death.

The most unforgettable event of that friendship is an excursion to Lake Winnipeg. For the old man, who had suggested the trip that is linked with a nostalgic vision of the past, the greatest satisfaction lies not so much in its realization, but despite the knowledge of his impending death, in the child's discovery of the unknown.

The intense emotions aroused by that experience draw Christine so much out of herself that she yearns for the closeness of her mother, symbolizing a return to a sense of innocence and security that she may, however, never fully know again.

The attraction of the unknown, even forbidden paths, leads to the anecdote related in "Le Déménagement." Captivated by her mother's tales of the pioneering day, Christine, too, is afflicted by "the family disease, departure sickness."[49] Instead of the elation the little girl felt when she discovered the grandeur of nature in the company of the old man, Christine, now eleven, unwittingly exposes herself to the hopelessness of the poor whose poverty Roy described so forcefully in *Bonheur d'occasion*.

The publication of *De quoi t'ennuies-tu, Eveline?* ("What are you longing for, Eveline?") in 1982 reinforces the essential unity of Roy's work with respect to her choice of characters and themes.

The story focuses on a bus trip that Eveline, now in her seventies, takes from Manitoba to California in response to her brother's mysterious summons to see him. The wearying journey turns out to be an adventure in friendship. As the strange, old woman shares her memories of Majorique and his family—whom the readers of *Rue Deschambault* know from "Le *Titanic*" and "Ma tante Thérésina"—her joie de vivre and lively telling create bonds of recognition among the various passengers. The tales about her own life and personal experiences strikingly illustrate to her listeners that these are essentially also the tales of their lives when they in turn draw on their memories. The life of Christine's mother has been so enriched because, without knowing the exact nature of her longings, she has been able to accept things in life as they came. Thus illusions or imagination have been more meaningful than reality or the realization of a given wish on many occasions.

Even the death of her brother before her arrival is not particularly sorrowful for Eveline. Her meeting of Majorique's children and grandchildren and the shared memories of her brother's life at the wake diminish the grief of his passing. Instead there is a fusion of the past and present, as suggested in "Le Vieillard et l'enfant" ("The Old Man and the Child").

Chapter Five
An Artist's Credo

La Montagne secrète (*The Hidden Mountain*, 1961), presents an artist's credo that is also largely Gabrielle Roy's. This novel thus supports Albert Thibaudet's idea: "The real novel is like an autobiography of the possible."[1] Just as autobiographical elements are deliberately veiled in the author's sketches of *Rue Deschambault* and *La Route d'Altamont,* "this summation of Gabrielle Roy's literary quest," as Jack Warwick terms it,[2] presents a painter as her spokesman to allow herself greater freedom. At the same time *La Montagne secrète* was inspired by Roy's friend René Richard, "painter, trapper, devotee of the great North, whose lovely tales made me aware of the Mackenzie and Ungava,"[3] to whom the novel is dedicated. Nevertheless, as may be expected, identification between Pierre Cadorai, the central figure of *La Montagne secrète,* and his model René Richard is by no means absolute.

La Montagne secrète essentially transposes the main outlines of René Richard's early life when he began his work and travels in northern Canada as a trapper in 1913 until the late 1920s when he studied painting in France. But whereas Pierre Cadorai in *La Montagne secrète* dies prematurely in Paris, René Richard returned to Canada where he continues to trap and paint. Since the early 1940s, however, he has devoted himself exclusively to his artistic career. Now in his eighties, René Richard has lately gained increasing public recognition.

Gabrielle Roy's essay for the René Richard exhibition in 1964 in Quebec City and *René Richard,* a richly illustrated volume in which Hugues de Jouvancourt traces the painter's northern period from 1910 to 1942, provide interesting comparisons with *La Montagne secrète.*

La Montagne secrète was received with mixed critical reaction. Those who found fault with this work generally expressed disappointment in the disparity between Gabrielle Roy's aim and its execution. Other critics, however, once again praised the author highly, as indicated by the following sample of opinions.

John J. Murphy asserts:

The Hidden Mountain has many faults as a work of fiction. It is not strong
enough in narrative and has a tendency to lack strength and unity, although
the author's reiteration of imagery among the three parts does contribute
toward a unifying effect. . . . It is the subject matter, however, as much of
Gabrielle Roy's vision as can be grasped. . . . which redeems whatever in-
adequacies are evident. Gabrielle Roy has attempted to capture the artistic
process. . . . Such a depiction should always be valuable and interesting to
the serious reader, who must bring his own creative power to the image
made by the artist.[4]

David M. Hayne, who agrees in essence with this latter idea,
writes: "If it is read solely as a piece of fiction, this is not a very
impressive work; . . . In reality, however, this is not a novel at all.
Instead it is a kind of allegory of the quest of the Canadian
artist. . . . Pierre's peregrinations are the archetypal voyage of the
Canadian artist or writer in search of himself and of his art."[5]

Constance Beresford-Howe believes that Gabrielle Roy's choice of
subject is too great to be treated in a single novel, but concludes that
the readers "have no cause to regret a failure in *The Hidden Mountain.*"[6] While Hugo McPherson finds fault with the novel's "coher-
ence and control," "flashes of great beauty" make *La Montagne secrète*
a "rewarding" work.[7]

François Soumande, on the other hand, has nothing but praise to
offer to Roy, affirming that he has never read such a "captivating,
pure, and highly colored" book and, as far as he is concerned,
Gabrielle Roy has achieved through her writing or art what Proust
has achieved for music.[8] J.-L. Prévost,[9] too, welcomes in *La Montagne
secrète* a very personal work of great quality that renews the author's
authentic talent. Jean Ethier-Blais[10] similarly admires Gabrielle Roy's
skill of style. Raymond Las Vergnas admires *La Montagne secrète* for
the "totality of Roy's vision" and the imagery that is both "marvel-
ously precise" and of a "captivating lyricism."[11]

The setting of *La Montagne secrète* takes the reader to the Canadian
North whose exotic nature may be of added interest, especially to
non-Canadian readers. Ultimately, however, the setting becomes of
secondary importance. Although the success and failure of Gabrielle
Roy's hero depend on the physical milieu as his inspiration, her use
of Pierre Cadorai as her spokesman for her underlying philosophy sur-

passes any physical boundaries. Similarly Pierre's actual wanderings are subordinated to his symbolical odyssey.

La Montagne secrète is a simple story peopled with few characters. Yet once again Roy uses Pierre Cadorai's companions to remind her readers of the "Canadian mosaic." Phyllis Grosskurth and Michael Hornyansky, in particular, have pointed to the difficulties that arise because Pierre stands rather alone. To them at least he remains unconvincing. "Pierre Cadorai not only lacks a home-life and a society, he virtually lacks a personality. He is essential painter, *homo pictor,* not interesting in himself, scarcely articulate, almost a zero," charges Michael Hornyansky.[12] Similarly, Phyllis Grosskurth observes:

The Hidden Mountain is one book by Gabrielle Roy in which we do not find the figure of the protective strong woman. Here she is concerned with man alone in the freest possible environment. But it is only through contact with other people that character can be revealed and developed. Even in novels in which the interior monologue technique is employed, the character reveals himself through his reactions to the external populated world. Pierre remains a cipher because there are no other characters on whom he can hone himself.[13]

The novel's three parts deal, first, with Pierre's awakening as an artist; second, with the discovery of his goal and first public recognition in Canada; and, third, with the artist's tragic struggle and quasi-victory in Paris.

While the critic François Ricard terms *La Montagne secrète* a *"roman d'apprentissage,"*[14] it does not follow the traditional *Bildungsroman,* that is, novel of growth and development. The familiar elements of confession and search for identity are skillfully attenuated through the introduction of the second model, or René Richard. However, Gabrielle Roy does not generalize sufficiently. *La Montagne secrète,* therefore, remains the search for identity of the artist without at the same time becoming the search for identity of the individual. Thus, generally speaking, in contrast to James Joyce's *Portrait of the Artist as a Young Man,* for example, the reader is always "distanced" from Roy's protagonist since Pierre Cadorai's artistic journey is not a mirror that reflects his own experience. Pierre Cadorai suppresses his whole being to art to the exclusion of the central issues of human experience, so that his formative years, family, friendships, and religion are practically ignored. This does not suggest that we find fault with the author of *La Montagne secrète,* but it is intended simply to point to Roy's original (though not unique) approach—especially in light of the "universal" elements in *Rue Deschambault* and *La Route d'Altamont,* as seen in the preceding chapter—and to account for some of the negative criticism directed against *La Montagne secrète.*

In Part 1, which portrays Pierre Cadorai's awakening as an artist, the reader learns that while fishing, hunting, and trapping in the Northwest Territories, Pierre Cadorai has been seeking his life's goal for some ten years. He ponders what his responsibilities to himself and to the world are. In the course of his wanderings he meets few people. Yet each contact is valuable since Pierre feels he gives something to each individual and in turn is given something, as illustrated by his association with Old Gédéon (who is identified only by his family name), his daughter Nina, and Steve Sigurdsen.

For some twenty years Gédéon, "the seeker after gold,"[15] has made his home along the Mackenzie river bed. Abandoned by his former companions and now a widower whose daughter has been lured away by a stranger, Gédéon still holds onto his dream. Irrationally he hopes against hope that the next day will bring its reward. He is all too eager to offer shelter and friendship to Pierre, whose revealing portrait of Gédéon that first evening of their meeting discloses much that has remained mysterious to Gédéon himself until now.

But inexorably Pierre is driven on. As a result of a chance encounter with Nina Gédéon, now a waitress, Pierre learns that this girl is happy simply knowing of the beauty of the Rocky Mountains she has seen on a picture postcard. Her great goal in life is seeing them with her own eyes. Only too conscious that he has not yet found "his mountain," Pierre envies Nina her conviction.

The image of the mountain affords Gabrielle Roy great potential for realistic and symbolic implications. Jung considers the symbol "the best possible expression of what is still unknown." Thus Pierre's first reference to the symbolic value of the mountain is most apt. Then, too, according to Jung, the mountain signifies a spiritual and mystic ascent to the heights where the spirit is present.[16]

Pierre resists the temptation to respond to Nina's affection, although he is not sure what drives him on. The trapper and hunter, Steve Sigurdsen, who later takes Pierre along as his companion in the Northwest Territories reveals to Pierre—the artist searching for his life's goal—the joy the artist can give his fellowmen as they attain greater self-recognition and self-understanding through the painter's art.

Steve's delight in Pierre's sketches of familiar objects and animals surrounding them is an instinctive response to art. Yet his acceptance of Pierre as an artist is neither immediate nor without a struggle for both of them. Being familiar with the Canadian North in its harshest aspects and most destructive potential, Steve is dismayed and resentful when Pierre disregards the importance of survival and therefore cannot truly appreciate Steve's just concerns for their welfare. Yet later Steve not only traps for Pierre's sake, when the latter falls ill— he even brings back paints for his friend as he senses Pierre's desperate need for them. In turn, Steve's unselfish actions remind Pierre of his special responsibilities as an artist. While Pierre owes his life to his friend's help, Steve regretfully realizes that they must separate, for art makes demands upon Pierre to which their friendship must be subordinated.

The first part of *La Montagne secrète* thus ends with Pierre's recognition and reluctant acceptance of himself as an artist. His goal, however, remains vague.

In the second part of the novel, that centers on Pierre's discovery of his goal, we find him once again alone. His is the fate of the outsider. Maturing as an artist, he wrestles with the problem of simplicity and perfection. Obeying the "summonses to his soul,"[17] Pierre must choose, or give himself to, art in favor of everyday life or his "mountain" rather than Nina and love.

Pierre's search for the ideal ends with his discovery of a "high and solitary mountain" in the northern wilderness which he names the "Solitary One or The Resplendent."[18] Thus the natural object corresponds also to the symbolic value of leading Pierre spiritually on to new heights. Henceforth, his life will be dominated by "his mountain" whose character he believes he must capture in its totality. The mountain's existence, Roy suggests, depends on the artist inasmuch as he must bring it to life and "reveal" it to others, if they are to see it.

Pierre's obsession with the mountain is both a blessing and a curse. Although he is aware of the risks to which he exposes himself because of the oncoming winter, especially since he is alone, Pierre decides to remain at the foot of the mountain to capture it in all its moods. However, by the time he is forced to kill an old caribou to sustain himself, Pierre is physically and emotionally so exhausted that as the hunter he identifies himself with his victim.[19] While this identification is due largely to his weakened condition, the memories of this episode will haunt Pierre—as will be seen later—to the end of his days. It should also be remembered that from the very beginning of his excursions with Steve Sigurdsen, Pierre had been ambivalent regarding their trapping. On the one hand he was eager to get the necessary funds to devote himself more to painting, but on the other he hoped the animals would escape their traps.

When after killing the caribou, Pierre finds all his belongings, including his paintings, destroyed by a bear, he in his feeble state interprets this loss as punishment. He believes he has failed the mountain since he has not succeeded in capturing its majestic beauty, its "exceptional splendor" to his satisfaction.

Despite, perhaps also because of, the mountain's "reproaches," and the belief that he alone may after all create the perfection of his inner vision, Pierre's will to live is sustained by the "command" not to let the mountain "die."

A short time later Eskimos from a neighboring village rescue Pierre and nurse him back to health. A missionary then succeeds in arranging Pierre's first public exhibition of his work in Montreal. Father Le Bonniec's efforts on his behalf culminate in Pierre's trip to Paris so that the self-taught Canadian artist may learn from the living and dead masters. Thus, as the second part draws to a close, Pierre is secure in his calling as an artist.

With Part 3 of *La Montagne secrète,* which focuses on the painter's tribulations and success, Pierre's journey that takes him away from Canada separates him also on a symbolic level from his self, leading to an identity crisis, which nevertheless ultimately furthers his artistic maturation.

Pierre approaches his new world with mixed feelings. Burdened by an overwhelming sense of responsibility, he questions how he may live up to the expectations of all those who have made this trip possible. For one thing Pierre feels completely uprooted in the unfamiliar surroundings. Instead of being able to respond to new stimulation, he feels deprived even of his memories, the source of his inspiration. Consequently all creative impulse is initially thwarted.

Pierre's discovery of the great masterpieces in the Louvre fills him with awe. Impressed by the genius of a Rembrandt, he is borne to new heights. At the same time his creative impulse is in danger of being foiled by an overwhelming sense of humility.

A chance encounter with the art student Stanislas Lane leads to Pierre's association with a master's studio. The teacher Maynard immediately recognizes Pierre's gift and accepts him as a student though he still lacks technique. Yet Pierre profits little from formal training, since he feels restricted in his freedom.

When he takes up painting again, he is haunted by memories of the Canadian wilderness. As he forces himself to paint Paris, as directed by Maynard, sketches of "his mountain" seem to force themselves on him. In his endeavor to do justice to his mountain, Pierre applies himself to reproducing or "creating" it to such a degree that he practically loses his identity.

Realizing that he will soon succumb to a heart condition, for the first time Pierre is determined to draw a self-portrait so that he himself might not be entirely forgotten. Quite suddenly he has the strange impression that all his previous work had not been an expression of his self.

Pierre's preoccupation with his self-portrait in his final days raises some questions in the reader's mind. Until now Pierre had refused even to sign his works because he considered them without value, as "insignificant," and therefore unworthy of being identified with him.

With the desire to leave a self-portrait, however, Pierre seems to renege on his earlier philosophy of self-denial. Ironically he mutilates this last work. Apparently the self-portrait in Pierre's mind was linked with his killing of the caribou, for it is distorted by strange animal-like eyes and mysterious antler-like protuberances, apparently "commingling the anguish of killing and being killed."[20]

Although Pierre defeats himself by destroying his self-portrait, Gabrielle Roy grants her hero a victory of sorts in his dying moments. The mountain appears before him in all its majesty. Attaining a perfect vision of it, he believes he finally masters it and transforms or re-creates it—although only in his mind: "But his mountain, in very truth. Freshly conceived, refashioned in the dimensions, in the facets and masses, wholly his, his own creation; a mathematics and a poem of the mind."[21] Gabrielle Roy's achievement therefore is all the greater as she transforms Pierre's ecstasy into another form of art: language.

In *La Montagne secrète,* as in *Rue Deschambault* and *La Route d'Altamont,* Roy insists on the concept of the artist's vocation. Thus the artist is given a "command" or "summons" that he must obey. That this common theme conforms to Roy's personal conviction is evident from her discussion of her own work.[22]

Often the exact nature and object of that calling are vague. While

for Christine in *Rue Deschambault* and *La Route d'Altamont* the desire
to write is largely a conscious choice, Pierre Cadorai "senses," rather
than knows intuitively, that he is to be a painter.

Pierre never experiences even the brief moments of confidence of
the youthful Christine. Obsessed with the shortness of man's lifespan
and the enormity of his envisioned task, he is overcome by constant
self-doubts, while at the same time his noble vision of art humbles
and exhilarates his soul.

The search for his goal leads Pierre to a confrontation or "encounter"[23] with himself, his fellowmen, and ultimately God. In the final
analysis, art at its best is a mystic or religious encounter—both for
the creator or artist and the beholder or listener. This is especially
evident in *La Montagne secrète*. In response to Gérard Bessette's persistent questioning regarding the symbolic meaning of the mountain,
Gabrielle Roy suggested: "Perhaps it is God."[24] Pierre Cadorai also
serves as Roy's spokesman when he expresses the belief that the artist's recognition of his gift is associated with a great sense of responsibility to make the best use of his talents. This implies a threefold
accountability. Although the artist may truly deserve the admiration
of his public, it does not satisfy him. His main concern is that he
does justice to himself and the vision that inspires him as well as to
God: "He [Pierre] prayed—to whom he knew not—that all within
him might be worthy of the task. . . . But had he at least the talent
that his soul exacted?" he wondered. "Oh, truly a strange task,
wherein one labors for others, but if need be, in despite of all."[25]

Pierre—the artist—believes that he has a duty to himself and others such that it renders him a slave to his Sisyphean task. When
death, which frees man of all responsibilities, tempts Pierre after he
kills the caribou, the commitment to something beyond himself—his
art—rekindles his will to survive. His greatest moments involve the
loss of his self in his art or a transcendence of the self and the creative
transformation of truths into art.

If the artist is to be spokesman and an interpreter for his fellowmen, Gabrielle Roy suggests through the character of Pierre Cadorai,
he must engage himself initially in the process of self-discovery and
self-realization. Thus, in serving himself, Pierre serves others, and in
finding his own freedom, the artist also liberates others and allows
them to become more human because he reveals to them channels of
communication with themselves and others.

Gabrielle Roy uses the image of the bird, interpreted by Jung as a symbol of transcendence[26]—to elaborate on this idea: Pierre "held within his breast a huge captive bird, he was himself that imprisoned bird. And, at times, while painting the light or running water, or some image of freedom, the captive within him would, for a few brief moments, break free and briefly try its wings. . . . Every man has such a bird held captive in his breast. . . . But, . . . whenever he himself set himself free, did he not, by that very fact, also set other men free, set free their imprisoned thought, their suffering spirit?"[27]

In light of the interrelation of the arts it is not surprising that Pierre should recognize in Shakespeare a kindred spirit who furthers his self-development. In Hamlet's monologue "Tell my story," Pierre receives confirmation of what he had sensed in the solitary wilderness. "Tell my story" is perhaps the yearning, often silenced, that every artist hears whenever he meets his fellowmen.

Again this corresponds closely to Roy's personal conviction, as indicated, for example in the Preface to *Un jardin au bout du monde* (*Garden in the Wind,* 1975). Like Jean-Paul Sartre, she firmly believes in the storyteller's power to transform and confer value on the simplest matter.[28]

At the same time Roy's underlying success in "telling my story" lies in the philosophy that "every man is precious and unique by virtue of what life has made of him or he of it."[29] By virtue of the artist's endeavor to interpret the mystery of life, art is not merely an act of self-discovery for its creator. It extends to the beholder, reader, or listener and allows him, too, to further his self-development. Thus Steve Sigurdsen acknowledges the most memorable images of his life have not been dependent merely on himself, on what he has been able to see for himself, but rather are associated with intermediaries who have had exceptional powers of description in colors or words and have been envisioned by him.

Pierre discovers for himself in the Louvre the magic of the artist's power of communication and transformation. In his *Old Man and Boy* Ghirlandajo's vision transcends ugliness. The most developed example of such artistic transformation in Roy's own work undoubtedly is her portrait of Alexandre Chenevert.

The concept of solitude and solidarity is yet another major theme in Roy's work. To fulfill his mission of communion and communication with his fellowmen, Pierre, the artist, is faced with the paradox of isolating himself. This closely parallels the dilemma of young

Christine in *Rue Deschambault* and *La Route d'Altamont*. It also corresponds to Gabrielle Roy's personal ideas, as seen in her as-yet-unpublished Carnets, for example.[30] Similarly, after the completion of *La Petite Poule d'Eau* where she portrayed Luzina and the Capuchin missionary—two characters with exceptional love for and devotion to others—Roy conjectured, "Perhaps . . . perhaps one must keep a certain distance from people to truly love them."[31]

According to Roy, art—being synonymous with commitment—therefore springs from love and is an expression of love for mankind. She notes in discussing her own work that she, like Pierre Cadorai and many another artist, is disconcerted when daily necessities force her to sell, rather than donate, her work.

Art, Gabrielle Roy asserts—both as to its source and destiny, is all-encompassing. Though it is the creation of an exceptional rather than a superior being, art addresses itself to all men. When Steve Sigurdsen, for example, sees some of Pierre's outdoor sketches for the first time, Pierre acknowledges the trapper's delight. He then perceives that his mission is to give joy and thereby hope to others, whatever their station in life may be. This presupposes an idealistic concept of man. Just as the artist is a guide for all, everything is worthy of his attention.

But the intensity of his emotional experiences distinguishes the artist from most men. This concept is related to keatsian philosophy: "The excellence of every art is its intensity, capable of making all disagreeables evaporate, from their being in close relationship with Beauty and Truth!"[32]

Art, Roy believes, is to be attributed largely to intuition or inspiration. Thus a given subject matter frequently involuntarily imposes itself upon the artist. This is also supported by Pierre Cadorai's experiences. "He was drawing near his goal, though always ignorant of what it was, knowing only that when he saw it, he would recognize it."[33]

The concept of the artist as a visionary is also particularly relevant. Thus, as Pierre begins a canvas, "He did not see, it is true; nonetheless he knew it in the same way as the dreamer to whom, while yet awake, there may be revealed aspects of the world hitherto unknown."[34]

Similarly, in *La Rivière sans repos* (*Windflower*, 1970) when Jimmy asks Thaddéus to do his portrait, the old Eskimo sculptor confesses to his grandchild born of a white father: "You have features and a nose of a sort I've never learned to make. And I'm a bit old to learn new things. . . . I'll learn your face in one of my dreams, that is always how I learn best. I'll wake up one morning all ready."[35] This, too, approximates Roy's personal experience.

Gabrielle Roy also believes that the artist's inspiration is to a large extent dependent on his roots or what he knows most intimately. This process frequently necessitates a temporary uprooting. In her preface to the René Richard exhibition (René was the model for Pierre Cadorai), Roy notes that, like so many artists, René Richard had to have his familiar surroundings in order to discover the material he carried with him. We remember also her comments on how she was inspired to write *La Petite Poule d'Eau* in France. Again, rather than speaking merely of Pierre's discovery of the mountain, Roy suggests also that the mountain reveals itself to the artist. He, in turn, will reveal it to others. Consequently memory plays a primordial role. We have already noted the importance of the past in Gabrielle Roy's entire work, especially in *Rue Deschambault* and *La Route d'Altamont*.

The artist's heightened perception frequently extends to more than one sense and permits the blending of various art forms, as writing, music, painting, and sculpture are closely interrelated. In art, Pierre Cadorai feels: "Linking things together was of its very essence."[36] Thus his pictures are often associated in his mind with music or the sounds of nature.

Yet a despairing Pierre discovers—as Picasso expressed it: "Every act of creation is first of all an act of destruction."[37] Initially this discovery had shocked and dismayed a disbelieving Pierre. Gradually, however, he came to agree that this was true essentially because the artist can seize only one moment on canvas, whereas the beauty of an object is frequently in its very multiplicity.

The concept of the artist in terms of rebel and collaborator, too, is of primary importance in *La Montagne secrète*. In his consciousness of his mortality and art as an expression of man's revolt against death, Pierre has progressed further than Christine in *Rue Deschambault*. Naturally Pierre is not alone in this regard. Roy reminds us in *La Montagne secrète* through Father Le Bonniec of Camus's reference to art in terms of a protest. It is, of course, a philosophy that has been espoused through the ages.

The revolt against death paradoxically culminates also in the art-

ist's "secret collaboration" with God, as Pierre sees it. When the Eskimo Orok looks at Pierre's mountain sketches, he acknowledges
with awe the artist's "divinity." Indeed, Pierre's encounter with the
mountain satisfied him that "our great mysterious dreams of beauty
and of love do not play us false. It is not to make mock of us that
they summon us from so far away and hold fast our souls in their
relentless grasp."38

We recall also in "Ma Grand-mère toute-puissante" in *Rue
Deschambault* little Christine's association of her "almighty Grandmother" with God and the old woman's acknowledgment that
throughout her life she helped with God's work.

The principle of collaboration is largely derived from the notion of
art in terms of "creation" versus "re-creation" or "projection" versus
"reflection." Gabrielle Roy considers imitation the most primitive
step in the creative process. An authentic work of art must transcend
objective reality.39 Thus, just as Roy notes that the painter Paul
Lemieux projected himself into his portrait of her, Pierre Cadorai's
mountain becomes "his mountain, in very truth."40

Inasmuch as art implies interpretation, transformation, education,
and the search for perfection, Roy's choice of a mountain—"the Solitary One or The Resplendent"—to apotheosize Pierre's ideal is most
auspicious. And Gabrielle Roy—the writer—succeeds in "creating"
for our mind's eyes the vision that had determined Pierre's life
achievement of which ironically lies at the root of his failure: "The
mountain of his imagination had almost nothing in common with the
mountain in Ungava. . . . And certainly it was no longer any question of who had the better succeeded with his mountain, God or
Pierre, but merely that he, Pierre, had likewise created."41

Measuring his accomplishments against his expectations, the artist
is always compelled to begin his task again. His search for perfection
translates itself also in the aspiration to create a simple masterpiece
that embodies its creator's entire vision. In this respect, Pierre
Cadorai feels, the painter is at a greater disadvantage than the writer.
Discovering *The Complete Works of Shakespeare* in one volume, he is en-
vious that he, as a painter, would be forever inevitably denied the
opportunity of offering to others his life's works in a form that is easily accessible and portable.

In discussing her own aspirations, Roy observes to Donald Cameron: "I think a writer dreams, as Pierre of *The Hidden Mountain*
hoped, of putting all the subjects, briefly, in one undertaking. Of

course he never arrives there, and that is why there are always writers and always artists."[42]

Nevertheless, Roy grants Pierre Cadorai in his dying moments a quasi-victory: "For another instant his soul remained linked to the perfect work he had glimpsed at last. He must give it life, not let it—the work—die. That which dies unexpressed without a soul seemed to him to be the only death."[43]

Chapter Six
Worlds in Conflict

Gabrielle Roy's brief visit to Fort Chimo at Ungava Bay in 1961 led to *La Rivière sans repos* (*Windflower*, 1970). The novel itself is preceded by three short stories whose tone differs significantly from the major work. They are not included in the English-language edition.

The "Canadian" character of this volume is emphasized through its setting in Fort Chimo, Ungava, and Baffin Island. It is a harsh and forbidding land—yet not without beauty which especially an outside observer such as Gabrielle Roy appreciates.

"Les Satellites," "Le Téléphone," and "Le Fauteuil roulant" ("The Satellites," "The Telephone," and "The Wheelchair") bring to mind *Bonheur d'occasion*. Just as in that first novel indignation must have played a large role in Roy's motivation, the author's emotions are aroused by the plight of the Eskimos who are trying to come to terms with the white man's way of life. Roy's feelings are particularly understandable in light of the ideas expressed in her essay written on the occasion of the 1967 World Fair theme "Man and His World." This theme, we recall, was chosen to honor Antoine de Saint-Exupéry, the author of *Terre des hommes* (*Wind, Sand and Stars,* 1939). Roy's essay "Terre des hommes" interprets progress essentially in terms of human relationships. On an individual level this suggests to Roy a sense of belonging, of playing a particular role in the universe. On a collective level it affirms the author's belief of progress toward an increasing universal brotherhood. But in illustrating in "Les Satellites," "Le Téléphone," and "Le Fauteuil roulant" the confrontation between the cultures of the Eskimos and the white men, Roy concentrates once again on humanistic concerns rather than social problems. Also, instead of bitter invective, the author's criticism finds expression in sardonic humor that is altogether absent in the novel itself, *La Rivière sans repos*.

La Rivière sans repos has earned its author at once significant positive and negative criticism. The disparity between these opinions must be attributed largely to the fact that Gabrielle Roy reaffirms rather than expands her vision. As will be seen later, she takes up familiar themes—including family relations, social criticism, war, love, and life—which she now treats from different perspectives. Thus, as indicated below, while Phyllis Grosskurth and S. Swan have expressed disappointment, the novelist has gained in stature in the eyes of P. Sypnowich and Jean Ethier-Blais, among others.

Phyllis Grosskurth faults the novelist of *La Rivière sans repos* because it "illustrates once more her reiterated themes, her characteristic approach, her inevitable limitations. . . . Her writing has apparently ceased to be an act of creative discovery and has become a ritual of self-resuscitation."[1] Similarly S. Swan notes that "Gabrielle Roy has picked the most powerful theme in her writing career. . . ." but "it's an ambivalent work all the same—one shot through with compassion and strength and yet weakened by the devices of a calculating technician. Perhaps here, more than in any of her other novels, Miss Roy has been too much a craftsman and too little an artist."[2] Robert Dickson[3] expresses similar sentiments, particularly with regard to the choice of an omniscient narrator that precludes more serious psychological probings. For Pierre-Henri Simon, however, Roy's merit lies precisely in the fact that "the excellent Canadian novelist is content to be nothing more than a novelist."[4] In contrast, P. Sypnovich is delighted to "find" in *La Rivière sans repos* as in *Bonheur d'occasion* "jewels of moral observation."[5] Nicole Lavigne[6] admires the poetic style of *La Rivière sans repos* and the description of northern nature. The critic and novelist Paule Saint-Onge[7] appreciates particularly Roy's exceptional gift of empathy that brings about such a strong link between the fictional author's characters and the reader. Jean Ethier-Blais,[8] too, praises Roy for characters who reflect her warmth and whom she brings to life so masterfully, yet who are allowed to pursue their destiny to a logical conclusion without false sympathy or melodrama. Finally, Ray Chatelin notes that *La Rivière sans repos* is "written with the same simplicity, insight and sensitivity that have been the trademarks of her previous work."[9]

"Le Téléphone," "Les Satellites," and "Le Fauteuil Roulant"

The Eskimos' fate suggests a tragic reversal of progress. Though they have been largely deprived of their old traditions and values, the new ways and morals remain essentially foreign and senseless to them, frequently occasioning bewilderment, sadness, though sometimes even laughter.

Although modern conveniences such as the telephone may be found in the far North, their use—or rather misuse—occasionally provokes humorous situations as Gabrielle Roy relates in a lighthearted, yet critical, vein in "Le Téléphone." When Barnaby acquires a telephone in his tent, he is naturally eager to make use of it. But he soon realizes how little he and his friends are used to the white man's small talk.

To pass the time, the idle Barnaby, like many other Eskimos, resorts therefore to pestering various white people with trivial calls. When his identity is discovered by the village priest, Barnaby is ashamed of his unseemly conduct and disgusted with himself. The priest impresses upon Barnaby how often many people become slaves to the telephone—always anticipating calls and wondering what calls they could have missed during their absences, but that the telephone cannot help to relieve boredom for long. He convinces Barnaby that he would find far greater satisfaction and enjoyment by taking his canoe out again.

Barnaby, never one for half-measures, is suddenly eager to revert to his old self and freedom. He therefore packs all his belongings to join some other old-timers, unconcerned now that the telephone rings on unanswered.

In "Les Satellites" and "Le Fauteuil roulant" the theme of the meaning of life and death is poignantly reiterated. In the old days, Eskimos of different generations remind one another, death was regarded essentially as being part of the natural order. The weak and the old were allowed to die in peace and with dignity. Some, it is recalled, drifted out on ice floes; others found death in a snowbank. The white man, however, has ordered an end to the practice of abandonment that his culture regards as cruel, whereas the Eskimo considers it humanitarian in light of the quality of life.

"Les Satellites" deals at length with the fate of Deborah. When the forty-two-year-old woman falls seriously ill, she is prepared to die. The pastor's entreaties to live longer fall on deaf ears until he assures her that by going South for treatment, she will be cured and become her old self again.

The seaplane taking Deborah to the hospital naturally causes great excitement in the isolated community. The sick woman herself is enchanted when she sees a tree for the first time. By selecting cigarette-smoking and warm showers as Deborah's preoccupation in the hospital, Gabrielle Roy criticizes the white man's introduction of two contra-dictory elements to the Eskimos: soap for cleanliness and tobacco for sullying one's fingers and clouding one's ideas.

When Deborah sees in the hospital that the white people suffer the same illnesses and die just like the Eskimos, she becomes depressed because she is deprived of the hope that led to her presence in the South. When it becomes apparent that she cannot be cured despite her operation, she returns to her people. And as her illness pro-gresses, the Eskimos of her village conclude that it would have been better for her to have been allowed to die as in the old days.

As their thoughts turn to their deceased, who died on ice floes that drifted out to sea, they compare them to satellites that are forever revolving around the earth, and so death does not inspire fear. The pastor's visit causes renewed perplexity as he now impresses upon Deborah no longer that she must will to live, but rather that death will deliver her from all misery. Deborah's agonizing illness is so pro-longed, however, that she feels she is a burden to herself as well as her family. One night, therefore, she gathers up her last strength, as becomes evident from the tracks she left behind, and makes her way to the cliff where she must have fallen off into the sea.

With regard to its theme and the characters, "Le Fauteuil roulant" is directly linked to "Les Satellites." The protagonist is Deborah's fa-ther, Isaac, who has been paralyzed as the result of a sealing accident. A wheelchair dropped from a plane is a mixed blessing for the old Eskimo. More dead than alive, Isaac cannot make himself under-stood. Initially the wheelchair is like a throne for the sick man whom the women and children wheel around for their own amusement in-stead of the sick man's benefit, especially since the terrain is so rough. As the novelty wears off, both the chair and its owner Isaac— like a "deposed king"—become unimportant . . . Once he is even forgotten by the children who had taken him to the shore and left him out during a nocturnal storm.

Fear of the white man's bureaucracy, rather than true concern for Isaac's welfare, motivates the old man's daughter-in-law to take care of the dying man. Specific references are made to Deborah's death (related in "Les Satellites") that caused her people much annoyance since the white man ordered an inquest into her disappearance. Yet though the traditional way of dying may be deemed preferable by

Isaac and the community at large, it cannot be reinstituted. At the same time, the question as to why the paralyzed man's agony must be prolonged remains unanswered.

La Rivière sans repos

The story of *La Rivière sans repos (Windflower)* is that of an Eskimo mother whose love for her child, fathered by an American serviceman, alienates her both from her own culture and that of the white man. It is at once a very contemporary topical story and one of timeless simplicity and tragedy.

Part 1 (of three) portrays Elsa Kumachuk, a young unwed Eskimo woman, as she struggles to raise Jimmy, her son of mixed blood, in the white man's way in her predominantly native community.

In Part 2 we witness the failure of Elsa's endeavors. The fear that her conduct may affect Jimmy's total rejection of her culture leads to Elsa's decision to raise him in isolation in the old Eskimo tradition. But when the youngster becomes ill, the despairing woman feels compelled to seek help from white doctors. Elsa's failure to identify herself or her child with either one of the two cultures and her inability to harmonize the diverse values of the two worlds culminates for her, as seen in Part 3, in a life without purpose, prompted by Jimmy's rejection of his mother and his departure to the South, that is, his unknown father's world.

Gabrielle Roy's concern with psychological realism manifests itself in "flat" characters, to use E. M. Forster's terminology. Even in her portrait of Elsa Kumachuk, the character to whom all others are subordinated and whose importance is acknowledged in *Windflower,* the symbolic title of the English translation, the novelist frequently does not analyze her character's psychological motives and actions. Yet they impress themselves on our minds and become unforgettable, for Elsa is characterized by ambiguities and tensions that derive from a conflict she largely imposes upon herself. The Eskimos' world, as depicted in *La Rivière sans repos,* is governed largely by instinct and the wisdom acquired by adapting to nature.

The contrast and resultant conflicts between the Eskimo's and the white man's worlds are highlighted at the very beginning of *La Rivière sans repos.*

When an American soldier from the base impulsively rapes Elsa as she returns from the movies, this unexpected and involuntary experience does not arouse her indignation, for in her mind she links the incident with the events she had just seen on the movie screen. The fact that Elsa gives birth to an illegitimate child is hardly noteworthy for the young mother or her people. Moral considerations regarding illegitimacy are meaningless in her culture, so that she does not support the white pastor's efforts to have the father identified and held responsible for the child's upbringing. The Eskimos' world is one of Manichean values and a "laissez-faire" attitude that reflects a spirit of quiet acceptance rather than "quiet desperation."

Elsa's exclusive identification of herself as the mother of an exceptionally beautiful child eventually culminates in a tragic existence both for herself and her child. Ironically this is directly linked to her sensitivity and her desire to insure Jimmy's sense of belonging to one culture. Elsa's child merits special attention merely because of his exceptional physical features that clearly show his paternity. The villagers delight in the strange beauty of the child whose birth seems to them as extraordinary as the discovery of a new star. Jimmy's strange blond beauty usurps his mother's love, however, to such an extent that he dominates her life completely. Elsa's breaking away from tradition in this manner has profoundly alienating effects on her. Henceforth she devotes her whole life to satisfy Jimmy's needs—needs that are artificially aroused, ever-increasing, and insatiable. When the Reverend Paterson seeks to alert the young woman to the dangers of her unselfish, yet thoughtless devotion, Elsa is incapable of rationalizing her actions. But her instinctive, loving response, "Why, because he's Jimmy," is all the justification anyone could ask for, the pastor agrees, as this woman after all exemplifies a way of life he constantly urges the Eskimos to emulate: "Yes," he said, "there will be only one Jimmy, just as there is and will be only one Elsa. Though we're as infinite in our number as grains of sand, we are all, each one of us, a being apart."[10]

When Elsa becomes familiar with the white man's lifestyle due to her work in Elizabeth Beaulieu's home, she adopts this style for Jimmy's sake. But despite a certain attraction, it remains alien to her innermost being. Thus she soon experiences conflicts within herself.

Elsa provides for Jimmy unsparingly, but indiscriminately, everything the Beaulieu children have, whose father, Roch Beaulieu, a policeman, has been transferred only temporarily to the North. The parents therefore compensate the children for certain deprivations to which they are now exposed. At the same time the young mother seeks to give her son the joys and peace of her own childhood. This is epitomized for her by the Koksoak river. When she takes Jimmy to its shores, she fulfills "some obscure and marvelous duty." She is greatly pleased, therefore, when the boy reveals there a "gentle and dreamy" quality, as she interprets it to be indicative of his kinship with her parents and her grandfather Thaddeus.

Always guided more by instinct than by reflection, Elsa suddenly and wholly rejects the southern way of life when her well-meaning pastor entreats her to moderate her adoption of the white man's superficial values lest the child become ashamed of his Eskimo heritage in later years. Elsa's lack of steadfastness and tendency to exaggerate now manifest themselves when she turns her back on the white man's values to such an extent that she rejects even her family's selective acceptance of southern culture, such as the comforts of a home (instead of an igloo or a tent) and schooling. She flees to Old Fort Chimo, but soon realizes that she is no longer free to assume the Eskimo's traditional way of life. When Jimmy falls ill, she acknowledges her dependence on the white man and returns to the village.

The hospital scene is reminiscent of *Bonheur d'occasion*. Just as Daniel Lacasse is drawn to the English-speaking Jenny who represents for Rose-Anna the enemy, since her love threatens to deprive her of her child, two alienated worlds confront each other in *La Rivière sans repos*. Elsa feels compelled to go again to the other extreme by conforming blindly to the modern way of life. Ironically Elsa makes Eskimo dolls for the tourist trade in the South so she can afford to buy herself the white man's amenities.

Nevertheless, the restless woman cannot fully suppress her nature and becomes increasingly anguished. Her people traditionally had been unconcerned with the past and the future. But for Elsa, as for Florentine in *Bonheur d'occasion*, time is an enemy: "If she tried to look into the still cloudy future, she felt that it was bound to separate her more and more from her real nature and would sweep her finally far from herself. She could form no clear picture of where she was going. . . . She was condemned, she saw, to move farther and farther into the unknown."[11] But as the years pass, Elsa becomes more and more embittered. The child that had always been the center of her universe becomes ashamed of his dark-complexioned mother, upon whom he looks as a "stranger," and his Eskimo heritage, and is eager to find his father.

When the adolescent Jimmy disappears, Elsa has reached the abyss of her emotional tragedy. Incapable of projecting herself or rebelling against her fate, she withdraws into herself, becomes completely apathetic, and loses all purpose in life. Nevertheless, she is strangely content. As the white man's culture loses its hold on her, the so-called security associated with steady employment and a salary becomes meaningless for Elsa. She simply works enough to satisfy her most basic needs for food and shelter, intent on attaining the right to do nothing except sitting by the riverside to be borne along by dreams of freedom.

Elsa's return to nature entails also a reconciliation with herself. At the same time her unfailing love for Jimmy is so intense that she feels secure in the knowledge that he will one day return to her.

The novel's final image of Elsa on the shore of the Koksoak skillfully highlights her solitude and fragility emphasized in the English title. "She would . . . gather up a few trifles . . . some of those plant filaments, as delicate, soft, and silky as the hair of a child, that are made to carry migratory seeds far into the distance. She would separate them strand by strand and blow upon them, her ruined face smiling to see them rise and scatter in the evening."[12] P. Sypnovich justifiably praises Gabrielle Roy: "In the final scene, the title scene, the reader is subjected to an emotional catharsis of remarkable power. The scene would be pure sentimentality except that it is quite true, and it makes *Windflower* a useful novel for those who need strength to go on."[13]

For Elsa the conflict between two alien worlds is largely self-imposed. Jimmy, because of his mixed blood, on the other hand, cannot choose either world, for basically he is at home in neither.

From birth Jimmy's strange physical features single him out among the villagers. They succumb so much to the boy's charm that they readily grant him all his wishes. But his admirers unwittingly sow the seeds of his tragic future. The child's privileged position inevitably leads to his involuntary tyranny (that destroys his mother as she seeks to subordinate her entire being to her only child) and ultimately grief as he comes to feel superior to the Eskimos.

Yet when quite young, Jimmy had shown, much to his mother's delight, an extraordinary sensitivity to nature. And when Elsa joins her uncle Ian in Old Fort Chimo, the old man readily shares with Jimmy his understanding and knowledge of the rugged tundra acquired over the years, when Jimmy lives up to the older man's expectations. But the troubled boy cannot escape the knowledge of his difference. Thaddéus, for example, maintains he cannot sculpt his grandchild's unfamiliar features. And Jimmy's questions regarding his identity cannot be satisfied for long by the wise man's sibylic answer that Jimmy's presence among the Eskimos is for their "joy" and their "perpetual astonishment."

Over the years Jimmy's sense of shame of Elsa and his Eskimo heritage increases so that the adolescent comes to regard his adoring mother as a stranger. Love then dictates Elsa to embellish the story of her union with the unknown soldier. Involuntarily she thus spurs the boy on to search for his unknown father somewhere in Mississippi.

Although Jimmy's first attempt to flee from home is short-lived and he is returned to her because he is under age, Elsa rightly senses that her son is forever lost to her. Nevertheless, Jimmy's second and apparently permanent disappearance at the age of sixteen gives Elsa a sense of pride. On the one hand, she admires Americans and knows that her son sees the United States as a paradise; on the other hand, she firmly believes that he will return to her one day to share his discoveries with her just as he always did as a child.

The Koksoak river provides Elsa with a natural—but ambivalent—symbol of life accentuated in the original title. From childhood she associated its rhythmic sounds with peace and happiness (sentiments that Monsieur Roch Beaulieu, too, experiences there). She therefore takes Jimmy to its shores to share these feelings with him. The Koksoak represents also a realistic and symbolic division between Elsa's two worlds. When she has abandoned the white man's way of life, she delights in a sense of freedom, derived from the free-flowing waters. At the same time Elsa believes that just as the Koksoak flows toward an invisible goal behind the mountains, her life proceeds inexorably toward its ultimate goal. Like Tante Martine in *Cet été qui chantait*, Elsa seeks out the river shore to communicate with herself, to find self-reconciliation and to muse on the meaning of life. Again this reflects the author's personal sentiments, for, as she notes in *Cet été qui chantait:* "The river and life, both in motion, seemed very close to one another, though the movement of the river soothes us and life often gives us pain as we try to follow it."[14]

But in addition to the "pain" in life so prominent in *La Rivière sans repos*, Gabrielle Roy illustrates also the power of love. As the pastor had foreseen in contemplating Elsa and her child, human love "is, in the fullest sense, the mysterious road by which we are led to the discovery of ourselves. One, begun in poor soil, can bring forth a rare flower."[15] And the reader's final image of Elsa, whose whole existence embodies that truth, reinforces the figure of love.

The symbol of the Koksoak river imparts to man also a sense of the timeless quality of life—at least on a collective level. Thus concern with time is essentially foreign to Elsa and her people who must take each day in their stride in this harsh climate. Thoughts for the future especially are associated with the new culture imposed upon the Eskimo, and, since they preoccupy her only for Jimmy's sake, they are readily abandoned.

Progress, that is, the white man's way of life, is viewed with much skepticism in *La Rivière sans repos*. Elsa's recognition that Madame Beaulieu's unhappiness and depression in spite of, or perhaps because of, everything that "progress" has offered, is decisive in her initial resolve to abandon the white man's ways. But Gabrielle Roy's indictment of "progress" is, of course, directed only against its dehumanizing aspects. In contrast to Elsa, the other Eskimos selectively accept foreign values and integrate them into their own culture. The key to their survival lies in their instinctive reluctance to change certain traditional concepts and relationships. Thus the Eskimos' adoration of young Jimmy does not translate itself into a desire to copy Elsa's example in the relationship with their own children. Even Elsa's uncle Ian who isolated himself from the villagers, feeling that they have rejected too many traditions, treasures the Bible and books left behind by a white pastor although they present at times a real burden in his nomadic life. And Old Thaddéus, Elsa's model of revered traditions, once confides to the troubled young woman that a falcon's place on the cliff sometimes tempts him. But it cannot be, for the wind and freedom cannot compensate for a family and affection. Thus life with others in the "cage" is preferable, after all.

Gabrielle Roy, as already noted, frequently associates a close correspondence between her characters' personalities and their milieu. In the Beaulieu's opposing reactions to the northern environment, however, the novelist elaborates on a broader, realistic perspective. Whereas Elizabeth Beaulieu becomes more and more depressed by the unfamiliar bleak physical surroundings, Roch Beaulieu feels—much like the Capuchin priest in *La Petite Poule d'Eau*—much freer and responds to nature. He is attracted to the barrenness because it suggests to him an openness and genuine quality that, he thinks, is no longer found among people characterized by hidden rivalry and self-imposed masks to hide their true feelings. Convinced that neither he nor his wife can be faulted for their sentiments, the policeman intends to transfer back to the South. Roch Beaulieu's status in the community naturally renders his criticism of his, that is, the white man's culture particularly effective. He is understandably reluctant to enforce the law of compulsory school attendance—especially since the southern program is so foreign to the northern lifestyle.

Similarly, the Protestant and Catholic missionaries serve Gabrielle Roy to propound certain views on Christianity and Western civilization. On the one hand, the Church fosters separation between the Eskimos and the whites by showing the same movies to different audiences; on the other hand, the Eskimos are drawn into the white man's conflicts as they are urged to participate in the ecumenical movement, although sectarian differences are meaningless to them. Christian philosophies are critically examined under the guise of naive, childlike questioning.

As in *Bonheur d'occasion,* war is deemed to have positive aspects— but now less for economic than for humanitarian reasons. While Elsa asks herself whose side she should take, the Eskimos are so removed from the battle scenes—physically and philosophically—that war is seen as a means of uniting peoples since soldiers will always leave children behind. "Thanks to war and the mixture of blood, the human race will perhaps finally be born. . . . a single family uniting all the nations."[16] Evidently Gabrielle Roy's voice is once again transferred to one of her fictional characters, for she believes that progress implicitly leads to a greater sense of fraternity.[17] Just as she bore a white man's child, Elsa images Jimmy in Vietnam and that she may have a Vietnamese grandchild. It is perhaps surprising that in this regard Elsa views this prospect only from its most positive aspect, that is, mankind uniting in universal brotherhood, heedless of her own and Jimmy's tragic existence in a kind of no-man's-land.

The idea of brotherhood ultimately overcoming worlds in conflict and the note of subdued confidence on which *La Rivière sans repos* ends, find expression with renewed conviction in *Un jardin au bout du monde* and *Ces enfants de ma vie* wherein Gabrielle Roy concentrates on portraying individuals representative of the "Canadian mosaic."

Chapter Seven
The Canadian Mosaic

Both *Un jardin au bout du monde* (*Garden in the Wind*, 1975) and *Ces enfants de ma vie* (*Children of my Heart*, 1977) are once again rooted in the author's prairie experience. These two collections of short stories with their central characters from a diversity of nationalities clearly illustrate Gabrielle Roy's consciousness of the "Canadian mosaic" that is represented in her work to a far greater extent than in that of other Canadian writers. In contrast to *La Petite Poule d'Eau,* however, where a strong sense of harmony existed among the various nationalities, the individual protagonists represented in *Un jardin au bout du monde*—French-Canadians, Russian Dukhobors, Ukrainians, Italians, Chinese—lead their lives independently of each other. This is related to the author's acknowledgment that the "uprooted" seem inseparable from life. Indeed, as Richard Chadbourne notes, "this uprooting, this exile, is an image of what she [Gabrielle Roy] perceives to be the human condition itself."[1] And Carol Shields remarks: "Behind the careful craftsmanship, the reader discovers a wide acceptance and a sympathetic vision of what it means to live on the untilled edge of society."[2] "Tell my life [story],[3] however, is the persistent summons to which Gabrielle Roy feels compelled to respond. It then falls upon the reader to reaffirm the author's conclusion, born out of her childhood experience. It is meaningless to speak of "strangers" for it applies to no one or every one. The differences separating men are far less important than what they have in common.

Un jardin au bout du monde

Un jardin au bout du monde (Garden in The Wind), that is "told in beautifully crafted prose," Paul Socken[4] observes, and that Gabrielle Poulin[5] considers one of the best books published in Quebec in 1975, is a collection of four short stories. Two of them, "Un vagabond frappe à la porte" ("A Tramp at the Door") and "La Vallée Houdou" ("Hoodoo Valley"), had already appeared in 1946 in a slightly different version in the magazine *Amérique française.*

"Un vagabond frappe à la porte" brings to mind "Les Déserteuses" in *Rue Deschambault* with the French-Canadians' attachment to Quebec and the idealization of their forefathers' homeland. Christine's mother in "Les Déserteuses" responds to her yearning by traveling to Quebec where she seeks out her "roots." In "Un vagabond frappe à la porte," on the other hand, the astute observation of his fellowmen and recognition of their fondness for "news" from relatives with whom there has typically been no contact for many years allows a tramp to introduce himself—as Cousin Gustave—to the home of the narrator where he then stays for some weeks. This childhood incident is re-created with gentle humor as the varying reactions of the individual family members are recalled.

While the father accepts the stranger without questioning, the mother remains reserved and even doubtful as to Cousin Gustave's identity because she cannot reconcile the presence of this man and her husband's earlier accounts, however vague, of his relatives. But she, too, is taken in when Cousin Gustave, having sensed her piety and always ready to please his hosts, assures her that he has personally seen her revered Brother André in Montreal.

As the story unfolds, the dialogue plays an important role as it allows the author to emphasize that these people are not so much victims of Cousin Gustave's "lies," as victims of their own gullibility and imagination, for they suggest the essential information. The following is a typical exchange:

"Marcelline, now . . . did she ever mention me, sometimes?"

The man [Cousin Gustave] assured him warmly: "Oh, for sure! She often talked about her brother . . ."

"Arthur." My father completed the sentence.

"That's it, Arthur."[6]

But when Cousin Gustave senses later that his stories no longer hold their earlier fascination for his hosts, he disappears without even bidding them good-bye. Except for the occasional postcard with news from other relatives whom he had promised to look up on his travels, Cousin Gustave's visit is almost forgotten until he reappears—a sick man—many years later.

Now, to everyone's astonishment, the delirious man betrays himself:

"I'm Barthélemy, . . . Son of your brother Alcide. I come from Saint-Jérôme." . . .

Then again: "Come on! You don't know me? I'm Honoré, Old man Phidime's boy, the one they thought was dead. I'm his Honoré!"[7]

When the father then seeks out their distant neighbor to telephone for a doctor, he is outraged when he discovers that the police have started an enquiry about this "imposter" who passed himself off throughout his travels as a member of the particular family he happened to visit.

"Où iras-tu Sam Lee Wong?" ("Where will you go Sam Lee Wong?") is an imaginative account of a Chinese immigrant's lonely existence in his restaurant in Horizon, Saskatchewan.

A misunderstanding, arising out of his linguistic and cultural isolation, forces Sam Lee Wong to leave the village that had been his home for some twenty-five years when he must give up his restaurant business. Unable to explain to a friend that he intends to open up a laundry shop in Horizon, he is given a surprise going-away party on the assumption that he plans to retire and return to China. Of course, the party can bring little joy to the disconcerted Sam Lee Wong. Now he is the victim of a puzzling village custom. Whenever public affection or honor was shown to someone like him, an "unwritten law" seemed to dictate his departure.

Sam Lee Wong then settles quite at random in Sweet Clover, Saskatchewan, for its hills remind him once again of his homeland. As already suggested by the settlements' names, ironic overtones frequently enter into the author's description of the daily happenings and customs of small towns with emphasis on stereotyping.

"La Vallée Houdou" briefly relates how a group of Dukhobors decides on the site of their new settlement in a most unfavorable location, much to the consternation of their Canadian guides. This selection may be considered a forerunner of "Le Puits de Dunrea" in *Rue Deschambault* that clarifies further some of the sect's psychological and religious characteristics.

The memory of a little garden on the open prairie occasions Gabrielle Roy to muse on the life of Marta Yaremko in "Un jardin au bout du monde," the story that provides the title for the book. Like "La Vallée Houdou," this story dramatically illustrates how the confrontation with the new land resembles also a confrontation with the self.

Dominant Themes of
Un jardin au bout du monde

The art of storytelling is not only one that Gabrielle Roy admires in others, but also one in which she herself excels, as evidenced in this and earlier collections of short stories. In addition to the simple entertainment of *Un jardin au bout du monde* which Robert Tremblay justly characterizes as "profound, pathetic and in some respects prophetic,"[8] these stories serve to reintroduce a number of themes, including dreams and reality, solitude and communication, and the meaning of life.

Dreams, in their broadest possible interpretation, as in *Bonheur d'occasion,* again play a major role in these people's lives. For the artist this may mean that the world he creates may be more real, more true than reality itself. Thus, in telling the story of Marta Yaremko, the first-person narrator reflects on the writer's craft and recalls that earlier in her career she had asked herself somewhat despondently: "Why bother inventing yet another story—would it be closer to reality than the facts themselves?" And even now she sometimes thinks that little garden "was a dream and nothing more!"[9]

Similarly, Gabrielle Roy notes in her preface to *Un jardin au bout du monde* regarding Sam Lee Wong: "I might be the only one who had imagined his life and, as a result, was able to give it reality."[10]

The Dukhobors' persistent search for a particular type of location is based on their past. Ultimately their choice of the Hoodoo Valley with its "mountains in the distance, a river in the grass" is based on a "mirage and trumpery." To their uncomprehending guides these settlers try to explain their elation. However illusory the mountains themselves may be, the intensity of the Dukhobors' faith alone matters. This brings to mind Alexandre Chenevert's observation that the mere knowledge of the existence of a "paradise" like Lac Vert satisfies his yearning for it. We recall also how Pierre Cadorai, still searching for his goal, envied Nina Gédéon for her conviction that she will behold one day her mountains in *La Montagne secrète.*

In "Un vagabond frappe à la porte" the destruction of his dreams regarding his relatives causes the father to react violently to "Cousin Gustave's" deception. The mother, on the other hand, in the end values the belief in something real or false more than the truth itself. Thus she can be generous to the sick man, and in bidding him farewell she can address him for the first time as "Cousin Gustave."

In "Le Veillard et l'enfant" of *La Route d'Altamont* Monsieur Saint-Hilaire surmised that life forms a circle, that the end and the beginning join and are fundamentally the same. This accounts also for the importance that people, like the Dukhobors, Sam Lee Wong, and the Yaremkos, attach to the past in shaping their future.

The geographical setting of these stories emphasizes the isolation of the sparsely populated, windswept plains. Great distances, traveling hardships, and the attraction of the unknown afford "Cousin Gustave" the opportunity to deceive his many hosts as to his true identity. Sam Lee Wong, who is forced to settle alone in Canada because of the country's immigration laws, is intent on saving his meager earnings so that his coffin may be sent to China, as he can hope to be reunited with his ancestors only in death. But solitude frequently takes on a more tragic form among human beings. A particularly poignant example is that of Marta and Stepan Yaremko. Although the couple live together, practically all communication between them has broken off for so long that they no longer dare to overcome this self-imposed barrier. Thus Stepan can show his concern for his sick wife only by caring for her flowers whose very existence had always aroused his hatred since her garden symbolized essentially their aloneness. Then, too, man's solitude may be accentuated by his feeling of separation from God. As the group of Dukhobors seeks a settlement, their greatest fear in the new and seemingly hostile land is the apparent silence of the Lord.

"A tremendous merry-go-round where no one ever understood anyone else"[11] is the vision of the world proclaimed by an acquaintance of the Chinese immigrant in "Où iras-tu Sam Lee Wong?" What is the meaning of life then and what is our identity are questions that Roy's characters ask themselves explicitly, as in the case of Marta Yaremko, or on whose behalf these problems are raised implicitly. As Roy always chooses symbols that arise naturally from her environment, as far as Sam Lee Wong is concerned, his whole life is envisioned in terms of "one long drought" that has been interrupted only momentarily by occasional contacts with others. The language barrier is but one aspect of that isolation. For Marta Yaremko the vague sensation of impending death may initiate, or at least precipitate, reflections of her existence. The Yaremkos' incomplete mastery of English aggravates their failure to express fully their real selves even with their children. "A long, dry, windy day" is Stepan Yaremko's perception of his life, and so he cannot comprehend his wife's love for life. No doubt their opposing natures that had once attracted the young lovers largely lie at the root of Marta's sad acknowledgment that only in youth was she herself. At the present time, therefore, Marta, motivated by sentiments of love, being responsible and having to give an account of her life before God, sees the meaning of her life in her garden that she brings to flower. She then offers the fruits of her labor as her legacy to the icons in the tiny, deserted chapel.

Ces enfants de ma vie

Ces enfants de ma vie (Children of My Heart) presents the typical admixture of autobiography to short stories that characterizes Rue Deschambault and La Route d'Altamont. The collection, divided into three parts, achieves unity through the first-person narrator. As Louis Dudek has pointed out, this mode suggests "there is a special commitment to life, a direct personal involvement of the writer with the meaning of his work."[12] This involvement has earned Gabrielle Roy once again high praise. For example, Yves Thériault, one of Quebec's most prolific writers and a fellow member of the Royal Society of Canada, admires above all "the discreet beauty of her style." He also expresses the "wish that he could write like Gabrielle Roy and love and understand her characters as she does."[13] Gilles Marcotte,[14] too, admires Ces enfants de ma vie for its passionate, moving, and deeply personal qualities. Both he and Thuong Vuong Riddick[15] find this work far superior to Bonheur d'occasion despite the latter novel's considerable merits because this collection of short stories has been enriched by the experiences of a lifetime. Gabrielle Poulin[16] and William French[17] express similar sentiments. The narrator, a teacher as in La Petite Poule d'Eau, looks back on some of the earliest experiences of her career and sketches pupils of different ethnic groups. The milieu of these children's homes is generally as impoverished as that of Bonheur d'occasion. But the emotional foundation of Ces enfants de ma vie is, as Jacques Godbout says, one of "gentleness," "sensitivity," "generosity,"[18] similar to the feelings that inspired Cet été qui chantait especially, rather than a feeling of revolt that was such a powerful catalyst in the creation of Bonheur d'occasion, Gabrielle Roy's first novel.

In Part 1 the narrator introduces with the first selection, "Vincento," an Italian child, whose emotions changed radically from hate to love on his first day of school. (In the English translation the individual selections are all untitled.) In "L'Enfant de Noël" the teacher remembers Clair and the poor child's despair when he could not offer his teacher a gift at Christmas like all the other pupils and the boy's courage in braving a storm to bring to the teacher's home after all one of his mother's "not quite new" fine linen handkerchiefs.

"L'Alouette" identifies Nil, who becomes unforgettable because of his extraordinary musical talent. The "little Ukrainian lark's" visit to old people's homes and hospitals brings to mind Christine's visit with the mentally ill Alicia in *Rue Deschambault*. Sensing the mysterious power of his singing, Nil is touched and frightened by the "terrible happiness" he has suddenly brought into these people's lives.

The portrayal of "Démetrioff" completes Part 1. The Démetrioffs, the narrator recalls, always seemed to stand out for their ignorance and inability to learn; and the father's brutality terrorized not only his children, but also the teachers. The author's "passionate need . . . to try and bring out the best in everyone,"[19] however, pays off again. The youngest Démetrioff's singular beautiful copying ability (though he cannot associate any meaning with the model letters) delights the illiterate father when he visits the school on parents' day.

"La Maison gardée," Part 2, concentrates on a portrait of André Pasquier whose compassionate understanding reveals once again Gabrielle Roy's personal stamp. His mother's illness and the home's great distance from school force this child to take on responsibilities far beyond his age and to give up school despite his love of learning.

"De la truite dans l'eau glacée," Part 3, with its portrait of the adolescent Médéric Eymard, completes this gallery of *Ces enfants de ma vie* in which the familiar themes of solitude, freedom, and love are interwoven. Here the wealth of Gabrielle Roy's warmth of feeling, one of the major factors in the popular appeal of her works, reaches its climax.

The story of Médéric illustrates *par excellence* Roy's premise that art is an act of self-discovery. As the narrator delves into the past and probes the ambivalent relationship between teacher and student, there is ample evidence of self-exposure and self-clarification. Then, too, the realistic descriptions culled from the author's observation of nature gain wider scope by investing them with symbolic values.

Médéric has a special fascination for the young teacher; partly because she recognizes that he is about to leave the world of childhood that she herself has hardly left behind. Obsessed by the need to achieve independence, Médéric takes his horse to the neighboring hills where he dreams of freedom and happiness. His teacher recalls how he fascinated her with accounts of his discoveries in nature. "I saw gliding over his face the joyous trembling he had felt at holding in his hands, tame and consenting, the most timorous fish [a trout] in the world; and I thought it would soon be his turn to be tamed, vulnerable as I now discovered him to be, if I could muster the skill to do it."[20]

The relationship between teacher and student is somewhat reversed. She has not yet reconciled herself fully to the fact that she may no longer return to the "lost frontier" of childhood. She therefore responds to the boy's invitation to share his "secret" world. The highlight of their excursion is their play with the numbed trout in the icy spring water. The spontaneous innocence of their joys of that day, however, soon becomes tarnished by the reaction of the suspicious adult world.

But the teacher, whose love encompasses all her students, suddenly recognizes that the excursion to the hills was like a prelude to Médéric's exclusive love for his teacher. Yet, although she herself remembers all too vividly her own torment of a first love, she cannot alleviate Médéric's suffering that marks "the death of a child under pressure from the man to whom he was giving birth."[21]

Chapter Eight
Summary

Gabrielle Roy has already been the recipient of practically every honor Quebec's and Canada's world of letters can bestow on its writers. She has also been consistently recognized internationally. Such official distinctions are supported by a large reading public whose numbers are considerably increased by translations—especially into English. Collectively Roy's works are now translated into about a dozen languages, including Japanese and Russian.

In 1966 Monique Genuist had eloquently commented on the dual aspect of Roy's writings: "Just as Balzac is French, Dickens English, Gabrielle Roy is Canadian," although her work is also at the same time of universal interest.[1] In the ensuing years Roy's imaginative writings have confirmed the fact that her work is not only quintessentially Canadian. In addition, because of her humanitarian concerns, her writings can lay claim to certain universal values. This is possible in essence because of her conviction that art is an enriching and ennobling force. Hers is a message that is at once simple and profound, a vision of life drawing on the wisdom of the past, expressed in a personal manner. In a literary world dominated by visions of the alienation of modern man and the loss of individual identity, Gabrielle Roy's idealism and faith in man offer renewed hope. Roy's work has not been directly influenced by her European predecessors. At the same time it is evident that it is akin to the authors she admires, including Selma Lagerlöf, Thomas Hardy, Balzac, Proust, and Antoine de Saint-Exupéry.

With the publication of *Bonheur d'occasion,* Roy became French Canada's "pioneer of the modern psychological novel," as M.-L. Gaulin has noted.[2] It may be somewhat difficult to appreciate the full impact of that novel in light of the fiction written in Quebec since then and especially since the Quiet Revolution, if we recall such writers as Yves Thériault, André Langevin, Jacques Godbout, Anne Hébert, Marie-Claire Blais, or Antonine Maillet. But in 1945 French Canada had been accustomed to view itself in the reflection of Louis Hémon's *Maria Chapdelaine* (1914) or Ringuet's *Trente arpents* (1938).

The outside world naturally tended to focus also on the romanticized image of a rural French-Canadian society, homogeneous in its language, faith, and traditions. *Bonheur d'occasion* was one of the first novels to portray the changing fabric of French-Canadian society under the influence of industrialization. Roy's uncompromising realism naturally clashed with the traditional idealized vision.

The sociological and political awareness underlying the composition of *Bonheur d'occasion* and the author's avowed consciousness of her French-Canadian heritage as well as her deep sense of identity with Quebec have aroused some criticism because Roy has not taken part in the political debate dividing Canada. But in contrast to a Claude Jasmin[3] or a Hugh MacLennan,[4] for example—whose novels largely reflect Canada's contemporary political situation—Gabrielle Roy perceives her role as an artist somewhat differently.

Being an artist implies freedom for Roy—freedom that expresses itself on the most fundamental level to be oneself and extends on a more superficial level to the choice of subject and style.

The artist must always remain faithful to himself and cannot adopt a particular stance demanded by certain social or political happenings if he is to be true to himself. This is all the more important because only then can the artist be true to others. Thus if *Bonheur d'occasion* and her later works are seen not from a sociological or political point of view, but from the broader perspective of humanity, Roy's silence regarding Canada's current political dilemma is understandable. She ardently defends the view that a prisoner needs both a lawyer and a bird: "It's futile to say which is more important, the man of action who fights for the rights of his brother, or the poet, the bird that sings at dusk between the bars of the prison."[5] At the same time Roy's position has earned her the highest praise. Jacques Dufrèsne, for example, suggests: "What distinguishes genius from the *littérateur* is that genius never adopts attitudes, while the *littérateur* exists only by them. In this sense, and in several others, Gabrielle Roy means genius."[6] Milieu is of course an obvious aspect of Roy's Canadianism. The west and the east are equally important, for while the past remains a rich and permanent source of inspiration, it is complemented by her new experiences in Quebec. For a true and complete image of Canada the overcrowded living quarters of the Lacasses in Montreal in *Bonheur d'occasion* are as significant as Marta Yaremko's solitary garden on the windswept prairie in "Un jardin au bout du monde." While characterization plays the major role in Roy's fiction, there is also a strong sense of place. At times detailed itemized descriptions are as significant as sensory impressions introduced to evoke an atmosphere and express a character's physical and mental state. A primary example is *Alexandre Chenevert* with its description of the city and the countryside.

Roy's intense power of observation of her milieu reflects itself also in her characters' dialogue. *Bonheur d'occasion* especially illustrates how vividly she can reproduce this element. However, Roy has used this linguistic feature less extensively in her later work to minimize the regional character.

As she weaves all elements of fiction into a single fabric, the story's plot, milieu, themes, and characters complement and reinforce each other. However, since interpersonal relationships and values do not change, in the final analysis psychological characterization or the universal takes precedence.

In her own mind Gabrielle Roy associates the classics of world literature less with ideas than with their characters. It is therefore not surprising that the focus on human relationships extends to her own imaginative writings. In creating an impressive gallery of "great" characters, Roy finds them among ordinary people.

The conviction that every human being has a distinct dignity is based on the author's personal contacts from early childhood on with representatives of the many nationalities that sought a new home in Canada. Her extraordinary empathy and love for her fellowmen are coupled with profound psychologic insights and a writing talent so that she conveys through her books her belief that the differences separating people are superficial since at heart all people are all alike. As Gabrielle Roy embodies her voice in those of her characters, her readers share Luzina Tousignant's joy in life as much as Elsa Kumachuk's tragedy; feel vicariously Sam Lee Wong's loneliness as well as Alexandre Chenevert's anguish; and the portrait of the youthful Christine is as vivid as that of her aging grandmother. Intent on seeking out the best in every individual, Roy has eminently succeeded in living up to her ideal of progress in terms of "rapprochement" of all and in her desire to manifest this in her works. Each of her characters is brought to life as the author responds to their silent yet imperious command to "tell their story."

Art represents for Roy a "vocation" in the strict sense of the word.

True art demands of the artist great sacrifices, for it can be accomplished only in a spirit of absolute dedication and solitude. Roy details this philosophy on a fictional level in *La Montagne secrète*.

In his creativity, Roy suggests, man expresses not only the essence of his humanity, but also his divine origin. The artist must respond to the creative urge within him, instilled in him by God or a superhuman force. And at the highest level the artist gives expression to God, as seen in the example of Pierre Cadorai's mountain. But Roy cannot be considered a Christian writer in a narrow sense. The idealist in Roy reminds us that everyone may be creative, as exemplified in "Ma Grand-mère toute-puissante." The impetus for writing springs also from a desire for giving oneself to others and sharing the truths that the artist has felt or understood.[7]

While Gabrielle Roy imposes high standards upon herself and devotes herself fully to her art, she also has certain expectations with regard to her public. Those readers who can approach her books with "confidence and impartiality," as she recommends,[8] will undoubtedly find the experience a most rewarding one. Donald Cameron, for example, probably voices the feelings of many when he concludes: "What I respond to in Gabrielle Roy, finally, is a quality that unites her child-like openness, her store of experience, her subtlety, her humanity: a quality I can only call wisdom."[9]

Gabrielle Roy· may be characterized essentially as an intuitive rather than an intellectual artist. Thus an emotional reaction frequently becomes the origin of her work. Indignation, for example, sparked the composition of *Bonheur d'occasion* which re-creates so vividly the lives of the poor in a Montreal working-class neighborhood. Even though precise documentation plays a large part in this novel, the experiences portrayed are obviously refined by the author's sentiments and imagination, which contribute in no small measure to the novel's success.

The importance of the intuitive aspect of her art also accounts for the significance of memory as the artistic impulse of much of Roy's imaginative writing. This is all the more meaningful as her imaginative pilgrimage to the past—especially in *Rue Deschambault* and *La Route d'Altamont*—is prompted by a desire for personal clarification in the process of self-understanding. "Invention" implies therefore for Roy in essence re-creation and/or re-constitution than "original" creation.

Thus on one level we may speak of two streams motivating Gabrielle Roy's work, namely, the present—as illustrated in *Alexandre Chenevert* and *La Rivière sans repos*—and the past—as seen in *La Petite Poule d'Eau* and *Rue Deschambault*. Generally speaking, a dreamlike atmosphere, at times a sense of illusion and utopia, seems to dominate in the works that have been inspired by the past, whereas an atmosphere of realism is accentuated in those works that are related to the present. But at times reality may become "transfigured," as Roy terms it, so that the dividing line between reality and illusion may no longer be distinct, as seen in *Rue Deschambault*. At times this distinction may even be forgotten by the author, for the unconscious is of major significance in her creative writing: as she has pointed out, while she "gives birth"[10] to all her characters, identifies herself with them, and gives them some of her personal traits, they also have an autonomy of their own. This may determine the events and the structure of a given work, as she indicated, for example, in her discussion of Rose-Anna in *Bonheur d'occasion*. In the final analysis, therefore, the question of reality or illusion becomes irrelevant because the characters she portrays are for Roy as real as—if not more real than—the models that have inspired her, and she succeeds in conveying their reality to her readers. The shift between the past and the present also recognizes the fact that the world of the self cannot be understood apart from the world of society at large.

In addition to the oscillation between past and present, or the prairie and Quebec, other significant dualities or conflicts characterize Gabrielle Roy's work. Rather than denying the essential unity of her work, which is rooted in her personality and its genuine and faithful expression, such polarities lend greater depth to her art and her concern for realism. Although the milieu frequently serves as a mirror for the individual's state of being, harmony with one's self and others must be found within oneself, as illustrated in *Alexandre Chenevert*.

On a personal level, one of the most dramatic manifestations of duality is suggested by Christine. She attributes to her parents' personalities her feelings of being a "creature of day and night." Another paradox that preoccupies Roy is that of freedom and solidarity as exemplified in *La Rivière sans repos*. The struggle between idealism and reality is still another distinguishing feature of Roy's characters, as seen in Florentine Lacasse in *Bonheur d'occasion* and Christine in *Rue Deschambault*.

An important aspect of man's idealism is the role that dreams play in our lives. Gabrielle Roy frequently uses them to emphasize both the uniqueness and the generality among men. One of the most touching examples is seen in the revelation of the secret tragedy of Christine's mother, as the older woman expresses the hope that her own unfulfilled dreams may be realized in her daughter's life and career as a teacher. And the example of the Dukhobors' search for a new home in "Hoodoo Valley" reminds the reader that the dream itself and man's faith may be all-important in man's search for happiness.

Again, while Gabrielle Roy truly celebrates life, death is not ignored. This is particularly true in light of the author's conception of "every life [being] a tragedy"—and especially that of the artist because of his exceptional awareness.[11] But the dualities and conflicts ultimately resolve themselves by the vision of life in terms of a cycle. Thus the end and the beginning, the past and the present are in essence the same, as the aged Monsieur Saint-Hilaire intimates to the young Christine in "Le Vieillard et l'enfant" in *La Route d'Altamont*.

Similarly, just as all her writing is perceived by Roy ultimately as an act of self-discovery—whether she adopts the first-person narrative of *Ces enfants de ma vie* or is the omniscient author of *La Montagne secrète*—the reader in turn sees in the fictional characters a mirror of himself. This recognition of the human bondage between the author, her characters, and the reader then increases his understanding of himself. And as the author endeavors to overcome her solitude, and as the reader responds to the communication he is being offered, Roy's faith in a fundamental brotherhood of all men is confirmed.

Like Pierre Cadorai in *La Montagne secrète,* she feels compelled to encompass everything in a single masterpiece. It may well be a task that has motivated every artist throughout the ages and a task that must always be taken up anew. And just as the artist addresses himself again and again to others, the public is content to respond to the communication that is fundamentally the same, yet is always being modified and refined by each artist's particular vision.

Notes and References

Preface

1. Gabrielle Roy, quoted by Joan Hind-Smith in *Three Voices* (Toronto, 1975), p. 88.

Chapter One

1. Gabrielle Roy, *Street of Riches,* trans. Harry Binsse, New Canadian Library (1957; reprint ed., Toronto, 1967), p. 131, hereafter cited as *Street of Riches.* "Et le bonheur que les livres m'avaient donné, je voulais le rendre. J'avais été l'enfant qui lit en cachette de tous, et à présent je voulais être moi-même ce livre chéri, cette vie des pages entre les mains d'un être anonyme, femme, enfant, compagnon que je retenais à moi quelques heures." *Rue Deschambault,* Québec 10/10 (1955: reprint ed., Montréal, 1980), p. 220.

2. Ringuet is the pseudonym of Philippe Panneton (1895–1960). He is best known for his novel *Trente Arpents* (*Thirty Acres,* 1938) which was awarded the Prix de l'Académie française.

3. Ringuet, "Conversation avec Gabrielle Roy," *La Revue populaire,* October 1951, p. 4: "Je ne connais personne de plus secret, de plus ennemi de soi."

4. Alice Parizeau, "La Grande dame de la littérature québecoise," *La Presse* (Montréal), 23 June 1967, p. 20.

5. Gabrielle Roy, "My Manitoba Heritage" in *The Fragile Lights of Earth,* trans. Alan Brown (Toronto, 1982), pp. 143–44, hereafter cited as *Lights.* ". . . un amour partagé . . . une inépuisable source de rêves, d'aveux, de départs, et de 'voyagements' comme peu de gens en convient autant que nous, famille, s'il en fut jamais, de chercheurs d'horizon." "Mon héritage du Manitoba" in *Fragiles Lumières de la terre* (Montréal, 1978), p. 145, hereafter cited as *Lumières.*

6. *Lights,* p. 145. "Chacun . . . le peignant à sa propre image," *Lumières,* p. 147.

7. See G. Roy, "Les Terres nouvelles de Jean-Paul Lemieux," *Vie des Arts* 29 (1962):39–43.

8. "To Mr. Vanasse and to my friends in the Association of Canada and Quebec Literatures" (typescript, anon. trans.), p. 4. Sam Lee Wong ". . . sans doute le plus solitaire de mes créatures jamais rencontrées ou inventées," "Lettre de Gabrielle Roy à ses amis de l'ALCQ," *Studies in Canadian Literature* 4 (1979):103–4; hereafter cited as "To Mr. Vanasse" and "Lettre," respectively.

9. David Cobb quotes Roy in "Seasons in the Life of a Novelist: Gabrielle Roy," *Canadian* (Toronto), 1 May 1976, p. 10.

10. Roy, quoted in Hind-Smith, *Three Voices,* p. 67.

11. See François Ricard, *Gabrielle Roy* (Montréal, 1975), p. 24.

12. This sentence has been omitted in *Lights.* "Les images les plus sincères de mes pages les plus vraies me viennent toutes, j'imagine, de ce temps-là," *Lumières,* p. 151.

13. Hugh MacLennan entitled his novel, portraying the relationship between English Canada and French Canada, *Two Solitudes* (Toronto: Collins, 1945). The term "two solitudes" is now commonly used to describe the frequent lack of communication between Canada's two founding nations.

14. Cobb quotes Roy, in "Seasons," p. 10.

15. "To Mr. Vanasse," pp. 2–3. "Le Québec, c'était mon passé indéniable, ma fidelité, ma continuité, une part de l'âme, nostalgique et peut-être comme inguérissable," "Lettre," p. 102.

16. Cobb quotes Roy, in "Seasons," p. 10.

17. "To Mr. Vanasse," p. 1. ". . . à travers le français celles qui avaient trait à l'âme, à la religion, à notre histoire à nous," "Lettre," p. 101.

18. Monique Duval, "Notre entrevue du jeudi," *L'Evénement-Journal* (Québec), 17 May 1956, pp. 4, 6.

19. See "Témoignage" in *Le Roman canadien-français,* Archives des lettres canadiennes, vol. 3 (Montréal: Fides, 1964), pp. 302–6; "Jeux du romancier et des lecteurs" in Marc Gagné, *Visages de Gabrielle Roy* (Montréal, 1973), pp. 263–72; J.-P. Robillard, "Interview-éclair avec Gabrielle Roy," *Le Petit Journal* (Montréal), 8 January 1956, p. 48.

20. *Street of Riches,* p. 151. "Gagner sa vie! Comme cela m'apparaissait mesquin, intéressé, avare!" *Rue Deschambault,* p. 282.

21. Hind-Smith, *Three Voices,* p. 79.

22. Donald Cameron quotes Roy, "Gabrielle Roy: A Bird in the Prison Window," *Conversations with Canadian Novelists* (Toronto, 1973), p. 130.

23. Ibid., p. 131.

24. "To Mr. Vanasse," p. 3. "Je sais maintenant que sans ce retour je ne serais pas l'écrivain que je suis aujourd'hui. Je ne sais pas ce que je serais sans le Québec. Je lui dois infiniment. Et tout d'abord de m'être aperçue moi-même comme je ne me serais pas reconnue ailleurs, et de l'avoir peut-être lui aussi perçu comme aucun autre regard ne l'aurait pu. Il m'a fait me cannaître peu à peu et aussi connaître l'essence de la vie, les tourments et la joie," "Lettre," p. 103.

25. Jean Ethier-Blais, *"Lumières," Québec français* 31 (1978):49.

26. Paul Socken, "Gabrielle Roy as Journalist," *Canadian Modern Language Review* 30 (1974):100.

27. See Cameron, *Conversations,* p. 139.

28. "Finalement, c'est le fondamental besoin humain de vivante chal-

eur, le désir de tendresse et d'échange fraternel qui me mena en bonne direction." Gabrielle Roy, "Le Pays de *Bonheur d'occasion*," *Le Devoir* (Montréal), 18 May 1974, p. 8.

29. *The Hidden Mountain*, trans. Harry Binsse. New Canadian Library (1962; reprint ed., Toronto, 1975), p. 4. "Tout homme est rare et inimitable par ce que la vie a fait de lui ou lui d'elle," *La Montagne secrète,* Québec 10/10 (1961, reprint ed., Montréal, 1978), p. 13; hereafter cited as *Mountain* and *Montagne,* respectively.

30. Gérard Bessette, "Interview avec Gabrielle Roy," *Une littérature en ébullition* (Montréal, 1968), p. 308.

31. "Recherche du temps perdu, donc, mais surtout recueillement et quête de soi." Ricard, *Gabrielle Roy,* p. 91.

32. "En d'autres mots, *Rue Deschambault* est autant une oeuvre d'imagination qu'une oeuvre de mémoire." Ibid., p. 92.

33. Eli Mandel, "Writing West," *Canadian Forum,* June–July 1977, p. 26.

34. Roy quoted in Richard Chadbourne, "Two Visions of the Prairies: Willa Cather and Gabrielle Roy" in *The New Land* (Waterloo: Wilfred Laurier University Press, 1978), p. 112.

35. Cobb, "Seasons," p. 14.

36. Roy, quoted in Cameron, *Conversations,* p. 140.

37. "To Mr. Vanasse," p. 4. "Mon mérite, si j'ose y prétendre, c'est peut-être d'avoir assemblé en mes livres des êtres aussi épars et qui pourtant constituent aujourd'hui une famille." "Lettre," p. 104.

37. *Enchanted Summer* (Toronto, 1976), p. 109. "Heureux ceux qui, du moins avant de s'éteindre, auront donné leur plein éclat! Pris au feu de Dieu!" *Cet été qui chantait* (Montréal, 1972), p. 175; hereafter cited as *Summer* and *Eté,* respectively.

Chapter Two

1. Alan Brown, "Gabrielle Roy and the Temporary Provincial," *Tamarack Review* 1 (1956):61.

2. Brian Moore, "The Woman on Horseback," in *Great Canadians,* (Toronto: Canadian Centennial Library, 1965), p. 98.

3. David M. Hayne, "Gabrielle Roy," *Canadian Modern Language Review,* 21 (1964):21–22.

4. See Pierre Descaves, "Un grand prix littéraire français à une romancière canadienne," *Le Devoir,* 20 December 1947, pp. 10–11.

5. "Elle a brossé . . . un tableau qui vaut pour tous les peuples du monde." Francis Ambrière, "Gabrielle Roy," *La Revue de Paris* 54 (1947):137.

6. See H. Gueux-Rolle, "Préface," *Bonheur d'occasion* (Geneva: Le Club du Meilleur Livre) 1968.

7. Hugo McPherson, "The Garden and the Cage," *Canadian Literature* 1 (1959):48.

8. Guy Sylvestre, "Bonheur d'occasion," *Revue de l'Université d'Ottawa* 16 (1946):220–21.

9. William Arthur Deacon, "Superb French-Canadian Novel is about Montreal's Poor Folk," *Globe and Mail* (Toronto), 26 April 1947, p. 13.

10. W. E. Colin, "French-Canadian Letters," *University of Toronto Quarterly* 15 (1946):412.

11. Doris Lessing, *A Small Personal Voice* (New York: Alfred A. Knopf, 1974), p. 6.

12. W. B. Thorne, "Poverty and Wrath," *Journal of Canadian Studies* 3 (1968):4.

13. McPherson, "The Garden and the Cage," p. 51.

14. Gabrielle Roy, "Germaine Guèvremont 1900–1968," *Délibérations de la Société Royale du Canada,* series 4, vol. 7 (1969):75.

15. Hind-Smith, *Three Voices,* p. 78.

16. Ibid., p. 82.

17. Roy, quoted in Cameron, *Conversations,* p. 133.

18. See B. Lafleur, *"Bonheur d'occasion," Revue dominicaine* 51 (1945):294.

19. ". . . une fresque sociale." Gilles Marcotte, *Une littérature qui se fait* (Montréal: H M H, 1962), p. 39.

20. "Le jeu d'échanges . . . s'établit entre les univers superposés: Univers individual . . . univers social . . . univers planétaire." Réjean Robidoux et André Renaud, *Le Roman canadien-français du vingtième siècle* (Ottawa, 1966), p. 80.

21. "Return to Saint-Henri," *Lights,* p. 159. "Un sentiment d'inutilité," "Retour à Saint-Henri," *Lumières,* p. 163.

22. See Bessette, *Une littérature en ébullition,* p. 276; André Brochu, *L'Instance critique, 1961–1973* (Montréal, 1974), p. 221.

23. *The Tin Flute,* trans. Hannah Josephson, New Canadian Library (1947, reprint ed., Toronto, 1958), p. 1; hereafter cited as *Flute.* "Ici se résumait pour elle le caractère hâtif, agité et pauvre de toute sa vie passée dans Saint-Henri." *Bonheur d'occasion,* Québec 10/10 (1945, reprint ed., Montréal, 1978), p. 11; hereafter cited as *Bonheur.*

24. *Flute,* p. 190. "Ses rêves étaient morts. Sa jeunesse était morte," *Bonheur,* p. 271.

25. *Flute,* p. 214. "Distinguée! Florentine était-elle distinguée? Non, pensa-t-il. Elle était vraiment une pauvre jeune fille de faubourg, avec des mots crus, parfois, des gestes du peuple. Elle était mieux que distinguée. Elle était la vie elle-même, avec son expérience de la pauvreté, et sa révolte contre la pauvreté." *Bonheur,* p. 303.

26. *Lights,* p. 168. "Le visage de milliers de femmes," *Lumières,* p. 172.

27. *Flute,* p. 143. "Il savait maintenant que la maison de Florentine

lui rappelait ce qu'il avait par-dessus tout redouté: l'odeur de la pauvreté, cette odeur implacable des vêtements pauvres, cette pauvreté qu'on reconnait les yeux clos.

Il comprenait que Florentine elle-même personnifiait ce genre de vie misérable contre laquelle tout son être se soulevait. Et dans le même instant, il saisit la nature du sentiment qui le poussait vers la jeune fille. Elle était sa misère, sa solitude, son enfance triste, sa jeunesse solitaire; elle était tout ce qu'il avait haï, ce qu'il reniait et aussi ce qui restait le plus profondément lié à lui-même, le fond de sa nature." *Bonheur*, pp. 208–9.

28. *Lights*, p. 169. "Jean Lévesque, personnage en qui j'ai incarné le refus des responsabilités sociales, l'égoisme qui conduit l'être humain à accepter les avantages de la société sans lui sacrifier la moindre parcelle de sa liberté. Jean Lévesque, je n'en doute guère, doit profiter amplement des conditions où la vie l'a placé. . . . Je ne saurais le suivre à travers sa vie; Jean Lévesque est si nombreux parmi nous." *Lumières*, p. 173.

29. *Lights*, pp. 159–60. "Cette petite femme du peuple, douce et imaginative, je peux bien vous avouer aujourd'hui qu'elle s'est introduite presque de force dans mon récit, qu'elle a bouleversé la construction, qu'elle en est arrivée à le dominer par la seule qualité si peu littéraire de la tendresse. . . . sans humilité et la force de sa tendresse . . . mon récit n'aurait pas eu le don d'émouvoir, car ce n'est vraiment que par l'offrande de nous-mêmes à quelqu'un ou à quelque but supérieur que nous touchons le coeur humain." *Lumières*, p. 163.

30. *Lights*, p. 171. "J'ai aimé tous les personnages de *Bonheur d'occasion;* je ne conçois pas comment le romancier pourrait ne pas plaindre et ne pas aimer la mondre créature issue de son imagination, qui, tout, incomplète qu'elle soit, le rattache au monde réel, souffrant et cruellement déchiré. Mais avec le recul du temps je m'aperçois deux de ces personnages me consolent des autres. . . . Parce qu'ils ont vécu l'un et l'autre pour le bien-être d'autrui, Emmanuel et Rose-Anna ne nous laissent peut-être pas entièrement démunis d'espoir." *Lumières*, p. 175.

31. *Lights*, p. 159. "[Rose-Anna] s'est introduite presque de force dans mon récit." *Lumières*, p. 163.

32. See Brochu, *L'Instance critique*, p. 233.

33. See Bessette, *Littérature*, p. 229.

34. Gérard Bessette, *"Bonheur,"* *L'Action Nationale* 18 (1952):55: "Gabrielle Roy semble incapable de mettre sur pied un personnage masculin, complexe, pleinement développé." See also B. Lafleur, *"Bonheur d'occasion,"* p. 295.

35. *Flute*, p. 236. "Il a pas eu beaucoup de chance." *Bonheur*, p. 332.

36. *Flute*, p. 266. ". . . l'assurance de sa propre libération. Libre, libre, incroyablement libre, il allait recommencer sa vie." *Bonheur*, p. 374.

37. *Lights*, pp. 169–70. "Je dois vous avouer que je n'ai pas eu le courage de le faire revenir, lui qui, au début de la guerre, était déjà allé un soir sur la montagne de Westmount demander à la richesse si elle ne con-

sentirait pas aussi son sacrifice à la paix. . . . Emmanuel est mort, il était l'esprit de l'intransigeante jeunesse qui ne veut rien de moins que la justice parfaite, et ainsi il était marqué pour le sacrifice." *Lumières,* pp. 173–74.

38. Paul Socken, "Use of Language in *Bonheur d'occasion,*" *Essays on Canadian Writing* 11 (1978):71.

39. W. C. Lougheed, Introduction to *The Cashier* (Toronto, 1970), p. vii.

40. Joseph Conrad, "Books" in *Notes on Life and Letters* (London: Heinemann, 1927), p. 117.

41. Elizabeth Janeway, "The Man in Everyman," *New York Times Book Review,* 16 October 1955, p. 5.

42. Margaret A. Heidemann, "Whipping Post," *Saturday Night* (Toronto), 26 November 1955, p. 18.

43. Gérard Tougas, *History of French-Canadian Literature* (Toronto: Ryerson, 1968), p. 158.

44. Andrée Maillet, "*Alexandre Chenevert,*" *Amérique française* (Montréal), 12 (1954):201.

45. Firmin Roz, "Témoignage d'un roman canadien," *Revue française de l'élite européene* 6 (1954):33.

46. R. M. Desnues, "Gabrielle Roy," *Livres et lectures* 32 (April 1951):199.

47. For details re these stories: "Feuilles mortes," "Sécurité," and "La Justice en Danaca," see Ricard, *Gabrielle Roy,* p. 76.

48. *The Cashier,* trans. Harry Binsse. New Canadian Library. (1963, reprint ed., Toronto, 1970), p. 102. "Il était pour ainsi dire innombrable." *Alexandre Chenevert* (Quebec 10/10 (1955, reprint ed., Montréal, 1979) p. 167; hereafter cited as *Cashier* and *Alexandre,* respectively.

49. See G. Dorion, "Gabrielle Roy," *Le Québec français* 36 (1979):34.

50. Tougas, *History of French-Canadian Literature,* p. 153.

51. S. G. Perry, "A Twentieth-Century Everyman," *The Scotsman* (Edinburgh) 111 (15 November 1956):18.

52. *Cashier,* p. 20. " 'Je finirai par mourir d'un cancer d'estomac', se dit Alexandre avec une certaine malice comme s'il devait atteindre par là du moins à une destinée tout à fait personnelle." *Alexandre,* p. 17.

53. *Cashier,* p. 140. "Jamais encore il n'avait entendu un être humain s'avouer heureux." *Alexandre,* p. 241.

54. Robert Weaver, "Canadian Fiction," *Queen's Quarterly* (Kingston) 63 (1963):129.

55. Heidemann, "Whipping Post," p. 18.

56. Gilles Marcotte, "Vie et mort de quelqu'un," *Le Devoir,* 13 mars 1954, p. 6: "Alexandre reste un thème, plutôt qu'un homme."

57. John J. Murphy, "Visit with Gabrielle Roy," *Thought,* 38 (1963):449.

58. Ibid.

59. Janeway, "The Man in Everyman," p. 5. See also K. John, "The Novel of the Week, *The Cashier*," *Illustrated London News* 230, no. 6137, 19 January 1957, p. 120.

60. *Cashier*, p. 92. ". . . le désir d'une île déserte." *Alexandre*, p. 148.

61. *Cashier*, p. 53. "Il lui arriva de se voir dans son propre coeur tel qu'il devait être aux yeux des autres: un homme aigre, contrariant, et qu'il eût été le premier à ne pouvoir supporter. . . . Si étranger, si hostile à lui-même." *Alexandre*, p. 78.

62. *Cashier*, p. 180. ". . . solidarité humaine," *Alexandre*, p. 316.

63. *Cashier*, p. 144. ". . . troublé comme s'il sortait de prison," *Alexandre*, p. 191.

64. *Cashier*, p. 126. "La présence bénigne . . . une certitude de Dieu," *Alexandre*, p. 215.

65. *Cashier*, p. 182. ". . . pour qui les hommes ne seront jamais supportables qu'à cause de Dieu," *Alexandre*, p. 321.

66. *Cashier*, pp. 198–99. "Comme ciel, il ne pouvait voir rien de meilleur que la terre, maintenant que les hommes étaient devenus bons voisins." *Alexandre*, p. 353.

Chapter Three

1. Mary McGrory, "Annals of the Poor," *New York Times Book Review*, 20 April 1947, p. 7.

2. Harold C. Gardiner, *"Where Nests the Water Hen,"* *America*, 3 November 1951, p. 130.

3. Gilles Marcotte, "Gabrielle Roy retourne à ses origines," *Le Devoir*, 25 November 1950, p. 18: "Il semble que Madame Roy, en retrouvant son pays, ait retrouvé sa joie de vivre."

4. Mary McGrory, "Wild Canada and Portrait of a Mother," *Catholic Standard*, 25 January 1952, p. 9.

5. Andrée Maillet, "Lettre à Gabrielle Roy," *Amérique française* 3 (1951):60: ". . . au-dessus de toute critique."

6. William Arthur Deacon, "One Isolated Family in Northern Manitoba," *Globe and Mail*, 3 November 1951, p. 12.

7. Janet C. Oliver, "Poetic Novel of Northern Canada," *Evening Sun* (Baltimore), 8 November 1951, p. 17.

8. See François Ricard, "Cet été qui chantait," *Liberté* 14 (1976):214–16.

9. See Jean Ethier-Blais, "Comme si la terre elle-même écrivait son histoire," *Le Devoir*, 11 November 1972, p. 16.

10. François Hébert, "Critique," in *Eté*, pp. 208–10.

11. François Ricard, "Critique," in *Eté*, p. 207.

12. Ethier-Blais, "Critique," in *Eté*, pp. 210–11.

13. Roy, quoted in Ringuet, "Conversation," p. 4: ". . . c'était

l'humanité sans la civilisation, l'humanité avant la civilisation. . . . une invraisemblable apposition."

14. Ibid.: "Chartres . . . le plus beau joyau qu'ait créé l'artifice des hommes."

15. Ibid.: "Ils n'existaient pas. Je les ai créés."

16. Roy, quoted in Cameron, *Conversations,* pp. 131–32.

17. B. K. Sandwell, "Perfection of Simplicity," *Saturday Night,* November 1951, p. 17.

18. Gordon Roper, Introduction to *Where Nests the Water Hen* (Toronto, 1970), p. vi. See also: Willa Cather, "The Novel Démeublé" in *On Writing* (New York: Alfred A. Knopf, 1962), pp. 41–42: "Whatever is felt upon the page without being specifically named there . . . is created. It is the inexplicable presence of the thing not named . . . that gives quality to the novel."

19. See G. A. Vachon, "L'Espace politique et social dans le roman québécois," *Recherches sociographiques* 7 (1966):262.

20. Gabrielle Roy, "Souvenirs du Manitoba," *Le Devoir* (Montréal), 15 November 1955, p. 17. "Une mère qui réussit son enfant, c'est encore la plus belle réalisation humaine."

21. *Where Nests the Water Hen,* trans. Harry Binsse. New Canadian Library (1951, reprint ed., Toronto, 1970), p. 55. "La connaissance donne la possession." *La Petite Poule d'Eau,* Québec 10/10 (1950, reprint ed., Montréal, 1980), p. 89; hereafter cited as *Water Hen* and *Poule,* respectively.

22. *Water Hen,* pp. 69, 75. "La nature, voilà ma méthode." "Du mécontement d'abord qui est la source de tout progrès." *Poule,* pp. 114, 124.

23. Annette Saint-Pierre, *Gabrielle Roy sous le signe du rêve* (Saint-Boniface, 1975), pp. 67–81.

24. *Water Hen,* p. 143. "La douleur du monde restait pour lui intacte, toujours indéchiffrable; mais de même la joie et l'amour." *Poule,* p. 243.

25. Paula G. Lewis, "Incessant Call of the Open Road," *French Review,* 53 (May 1980):822.

26. Anon., *"Cet été qui chantait," Châtelaine* (Toronto), September 1976, p. 8.

27. *Enchanted Summer* (Toronto, 1976), p. 19. "Mais les plantes sont comme les humains. Un groupe vit-il heureux dans un endroit, tout le monde veut y prendre pied." *Eté,* p. 30.

28. *Summer,* pp. 108–109. "Peut-être les lucioles ne vivent-elles que le temps de briller un instant d'un vif éclat. Comme nous tous d'ailleurs! Heureux ceux qui, du moins avant de s'éteindre, auront donné leur plein éclat! Pris au feu de Dieu!" *Eté,* p. 175.

29. Paul Gay, *"Cet été qui chantait," Le Droit* (Ottawa), 30 December 1972, p. 13.

30. *Summer,* p. 125. "Tous ne sont pas heureux au même moment." *Eté,* p. 203.

31. François Ricard, *"Cet été qui chantait,* critique," in *Eté,* p. 208.

32. See François Hébert, "De quelques avateurs de Dieu," *Etudes françaises* 4 (1973):348.

33. *Summer,* p. 5. "Aux enfants de toutes saisons à qui je souhaite de ne jamais se lasser d'entendre raconter leur planète Terre." *Eté,* p. 7.

34. "Ode à la joie." *Eté,* p. iii.

35. *Summer,* p. 91. "Si je pouvais encore une fois au moins dans ma vie descendre au fleuve!" *Eté,* p. 148.

36. *Summer,* p. 96. "Une créature tendue vers Dieu." *Eté,* p. 153.

37. *Summer,* p. 98. "Et elle était contente enfin d'avoir vécu." *Eté,* p. 159.

Chapter Four

1. *Street of Riches,* p. 6. "Certaines circonstances de ce récit ont été prises dans la réalité; mais les personnages, et presque tout ce qui leur arrive, sont jeux de l'imagination." *Rue Deschambault,* p. 8.

2. *Street of Riches,* back dust cover (English edition only).

3. Colette, *Break of Day,* (New York: Farrar, Straus and Giroux, 1966), p. 35. "Imagine-t-on, à me lire, que je fais mon portrait? Patience: c'est seulement mon modèle." *La Naissance du jour* (Paris: Flammarion, 1928), p. 57.

4. Robert Cormier, "Touched with Tender Magic," *Worcester Sun Telegram,* 28 August 1966, p. 10E.

5. See Pierre Lagarde, *"Rue Deschambault,"* *Les Nouvelles littéraires* (Paris), 29 September 1955, p. 3.

6. See Pierre de Grandpré, *Dix ans de vie littéraire au Canada français* (Montréal, 1966), pp. 91–94.

7. See Andrée Maillet, "Feuilleton littéraire," *Amérique française* 13 (1955):7–13.

8. Guy Robert, *"Rue Deschambault,"* *La Revue dominicaine* 61 (1955):316.

9. Ted Honderich, "Gabrielle Roy—As She Once Was," *Toronto Daily Star,* 12 October 1957, p. 28.

10. Miriam Waddington, "New Books," *Queen's Quarterly* 64 (1957):628–29.

11. Gilles Marcotte, "Toutes les routes vont par Altamont," *La Presse* (Montréal), 16 April 1966, p. 4.

12. David Helwig, "New Books," *Queen's Quarterly* 74 (1967):344.

13. André Major, *"La Route d'Altamont,"* *Le Petit Journal* (Montréal), 17 April 1966, p. 42.

14. Josephine Braden, "A Childhood in Manitoba," *Courier-Jouranl* (Louisville, Ky.), 18 December 1966, p. 6D.

15. François Ricard, *Gabrielle Roy,* pp. 94, 115.

16. Samuel J. Hazo, "Gabrielle Roy, a True Teller of Stories," *Pittsburgh Press,* 6 October 1957, p. 21.

17. *The Road Past Altamont,* trans. Joyce Marshall (Toronto, 1966), p. 145. "Apprendre à se connaître," *La Route d'Altamont* (Montréal, 1966), p. 260; hereafter cited as *Road* and *Route,* respectively.

18. Elizabeth L. Dalton, "New Horizons," *Chattanooga Times,* 11 September 1966, p. 17.

19. Marcel Proust quoted in Louis Dudek, *The First Person in Literature* (Toronto: CBC Publications (1967)), p. 42.

20. François Mauriac, *Mémoires intérieures,* (Paris: Le Livre de Poche, 1951), p. 4. "L'enfance est le tout d'une vie, puisqu'elle nous en donne la clef."

21. *Road,* p. 119. "Et si c'est cela la vie: retrouver son enfance," *Route,* p. 211.

22. Franz Hellens, *Documents secrets,* p. 151, quoted by Gaston Bachelard, *La Poétique de la rêverie,* (Paris: Gallimard, 1963), p. 117.

23. Willa Cather, quoted in Dorothy Van Ghent, *Willa Cather,* (Minneapolis: University of Minnesota Press, 1964), p. 19.

24. *Road,* p. 30. "Tous ces êtres successifs qu'elle (la vie) fait de nous au fur et à mesure que nouns avançons en âge," *Route,* p. 57.

25. *Street of Riches,* p. 71. "Sans le passé, que sommes nous? . . . Des plantes coupées, moitié vivantes!" *Rue Deschambault,* p. 121.

26. Hans Meyerhoff, *Time in Literature,* (Berkeley: University of California Press, 1968), p. 48.

27. *Street of Riches,* p. 15. "Mais, un jour, il me jeta le mot détestable avec colère. Je ne sais même plus ce qui avait pu mériter pareil éclat: bien peu de chose sans doute; mon père traversait de longues périodes d'humeur sombre. . . . J'ai compris plus tard que craignant sans cesse pour nous le moindre et le pire des malheurs, il aurait voulu tôt nous mettre en garde contre une trop grande aspiration au bonheur." *Rue Deschambault,* p. 30.

28. *Road,* p. 97. "Car je me dédoublais volontiers en deux personnes, acteur et témoin," *Route,* p. 173.

29. *Street of Riches,* p. 15. "Les parents peuvent croire que de telles paroles, bien au délà l'entendement des enfants, ne leur font pas de mal; mais parce qu'elles ne sont qu'à moitié intelligibles pour eux, les enfants, les creusent et s'en font un tourment." *Rue Deschambault,* p. 31.

30. *Street of Riches,* p. 20. ". . . une nourriture de plomb que je cherchais à avaler." *Rue Deschambault,* p. 44.

31. Samuel J. Hazo, "Gabrielle Roy," p. 21.

32. *Street of Riches,* p. 6. "Jeux de l'imagination," *Rue Deschambault,* p. 8.

33. *Street of Riches*, p. 87. "Est-ce cela l'enfance: à force de mensonges, être tenue dans un monde à l'écart?" *Rue Deschambault*, p. 147.

34. *Road*, p. 104. ". . . ce mal du départ," *Route*, p. 190.

35. *Street of Riches*, p. 54. ". . . une vie errante," *Rue Deschambault*, p. 107.

36. *Street of Riches*, p. 64. "Depuis, que nous étions en voyage et que maman découvrait tant de qualités à papa, il me semblait ne plus très bien le connaître." *Rue Deschambault*, p. 111.

37. *Street of Riches*, p. 69. "Peut-être pour devenir meilleure," *Rue Deschambault*, p. 134.

38. *Street of Riches*, p. 69. "Moi, j'ai tout de suite compris ce qu'elle voulait dire: quand on quitte les siens, c'est alors qu'on les trouve pour vrai, et on en est tout content, on leur veut du bien; on veut aussi s'améliorer soi-même." *Rue Deschambault*, pp. 134.

39. *Street of Riches*, pp. 144–145. "Le matin me semblait être le temps de la logique; la nuit, de quelque chose de plus vrai peut-être que la logique . . . J'étais partagée entre ces deux côtés de ma nature qui me venaient de mes parents divisés par le jour et la nuit." *Rue Deschambault*, p. 240.

40. Adrien Thério, "Le Portrait du père dans *Rue Deschambault*," *Livre et auteurs québecois 1969* (Quebec, 1970), pp. 237–43.

41. Louis Dudek, *First Person in Literature*, pp. 15–16.

42. *Road*, p. 137. "Un écrivain n'a vraiment besoin que d'une chambre tranquille, de papier et de soi-même. . . ," *Route*, p. 245.

43. *Road*, p. 14. "Tu est Dieu le Père. Tu es Dieu le Père. Toi aussi, tu sais faire tout de rien," *Route*, p. 28.

44. *Road*, p. 30. ". . . à tâcher de nous rencontrer," *Route*, p. 58.

45. Roy, quoted in Cameron, *Conversations*, p. 142.

46. Gérard Bessette, "La Route d'Altamont," *Livres et auteurs canadiens 1966* (Québec: Les Presses de l'Université Laval, 1967), p. 19.

47. Nancy Friday used this title for her psychological study on "The Daughter's Search for Identity" (Pinebrook, N.J.: Dell, 1977).

48. *Road*, p. 68. "Peut-être que tout arrive à former un grand cercle . . . la fin et le commencement avaient leur propre moyen de se retrouver." *Route*, p. 122.

49. *Road*, p. 106. "Cette maladie de famille, ce mal du départ," *Route*, p. 190.

Chapter Five

1. Albert Thibaudet, *Réflections sur le roman* (Paris: N.R.F., 1938), p. 12.

2. Jack Warwick, *The Long Journey* (Toronto; University of Toronto Press, 1968), p. 92.

3. *Mountain*, p. i. "Peintre, trappeur, fervent du Grand Nord, dont

les beaux récits me firent connaître le Mackenzie et l'Ungave." *Montagne,* p. 7.

4. John J. Murphy, "The Louvre and Ungava," *Renascence* 16 (1963):56.

5. David M. Hayne, "Gabrielle Roy," *Canadian Modern Language Review* 21 (1964):24.

6. Constance Beresford-Howe, "Canada's Best Writer, Gabrielle Roy's New Novel Entertains," *Montreal Star,* 3 November 1962, p. 7.

7. Hugo McPherson, "Prodigies of God and Man," *Canadian Literature* 15 (1963):75.

8. François Soumande, *"La Montagne secrète,"* *La Revue de l'Université Laval* 16 (1962):450.

9. J-L. Prévost, *"La Montagne secrète,"* *Livres et Lectures* (Issy-les-Moulineaux, France), no. 173 (1963), p. 24.

10. Jean Ethier-Blais, *"La Montagne secrète,"* *Le Devoir* (Montreal), 18 October 1961, p. 11.

11. Raymond Las Vergnas, "A la recherche de soi," *Les Annales,* 70e année, nouv. série, no. 148 (1963), p. 33.

12. Michael Hornyansky, "Countries of the Mind II," *Tamarack Review* 27 (1963):85.

13. Phyllis Grosskurth, "Gabrielle Roy and the Silken Noose," *Canadian Literature* 18 (1963):80.

14. Ricard, *Gabrielle Roy,* p. 105.

15. *Mountain,* p. 18. ". . . le chercheur d'or," *Montagne,* p. 26.

16. Carl Gustav Jung, *Man and His Symbols* (Garden City, Doubleday, 1964), p. 27.

17. *Mountain,* p. 106. ". . . l'appel à son âme," *Montagne,* p. 137.

18. *Mountain,* p. 102. "Le Solitaire, le Resplendissant," *Montagne,* p. 131.

19. See Gérard Bessette, *Trois romanciers québécois* (Montréal, 1973), pp. 185–99, for a psychological interpretation of this episode.

20. *Mountain,* p. 178. "Où . . . se fût fondue . . . l'angoisse de tuer et d'être tuée," *Montagne,* p. 213.

21. *Mountain,* pp. 184–185. "Sa montagne en vérité. Repensée, refaite en dimensions, plans et volumes; à lui entièrement; sa création propre; un calcul, un poème de la pensée." *Montagne,* p. 221.

22. See Cameron, *Conversations,* pp. 128–45; and "Souvenirs" in *Lumières,* pp. 141–97.

23. Rollo May, *The Courage to Create,* (New York: Bantam, 1976), p. 87: "Creativity occurs in an act of encounter and is to be understood with this encounter as its center."

24. "C'est peut-être Dieu." Gabrielle Roy quoted by Gérard Bessette in *Littérature,* p. 307.

25. *Mountain,* pp. 84, 120. "Il priait—ne sachant qui au fond—pour que tout en lui fût digne de l'œuvre." "Oh, l'étrange tâche en vérité, où

c'est pour les autres qu'on œuvre, mais, s'il le faut, en dépit de tous." *Montagne*, pp. 104, 144.

26. C. G. Jung, *Man and His Symbols*, p. 151.

27. *Mountain*, pp. 91–92. "Il pensait à cette impression qu'il avait maintes fois éprouvée d'avoir en la poitrine un immense oiseau captif—d'être lui-même cet oiseau prisonnier—et, parfois, alors qu'il peignait la lumière ou l'eau courante, ou quelque image de liberté, le captif en lui s'évadait, volait un peu de ses ailes. . . . tout homme avait sans doute en sa poitrine pareil oiseau retenu. . . . Mais, lorsque lui-même se libérait, . . . est-ce que du même coup il ne libérait pas aussi d'autres hommes, leur pensée enchaînée, leur esprit souffrant?" *Montagne*, p. 113.

28. See Jean-Paul Sartre, *La Nausée* (Paris: Gallimard, 1938), p. 60.

29. *Mountain*, p. 4. "Tout homme est rare et inimitable par ce que la vie a fait de lui ou lui d'elle." *Montagne*, p. 13.

30. See Ricard, *Gabrielle Roy*, p. 21.

31. Roy, quoted in Ringuet, "Conversations," p. 4: "Peut-être . . . peut-être faut-il être loin des hommes pour vraiment les aimer."

32. *The Poetical Works and Other Writings of John Keats*, edited by H. Buxton Forman (New York: Phaeton Press, 1970), vol. 6, p. 103.

33. *Mountain*, p. 170. "Il approchait de son but—il l'ignorait encore, mais assuré qu'en le voyant il le reconnaîtrait." *Montagne*, p. 203.

34. *Mountain*, p. 18. "Il ne le voyait pas véritablement; il le connaissait pourtant, à la manière dont se révèlent à quelqu'un qui rêve éveillé des aspects inconnus du monde." *Montagne*, p. 28.

35. *Windflower* (Toronto,. 1970), p. 52. "Tu as des traits et un nez comme je n'ai jamais appris à en faire. Et je suis vieux pour apprendre du neuf. . . . J'apprendrai ton visage dans un de mes rêves, c'est toujours ainsi que j'apprends le mieux. Je me lèverai, un matin, tout prêt." *La Rivière sans repos* (Montreal, 1979), p. 182.

36. *Mountain*, pp. 166–67. "Créer des liens était sa vie même." *Montagne*, p. 200.

37. May, *The Courage to Create*, p. 63.

38. *Mountain*, p. 83. "Ainsi donc, se disait-il, ne nous trahissent pas nos grands rêves mystérieux d'amour et de beauté. Ce n'est pas pour se jouer de nous qu'ils nous appellent de si loin et conservent sur nos âmes leur emprise infinie." *Montagne*, p. 103.

39. See Roy, "L'Arbre," *Cahiers de l'Académie canadienne-française* 13 (1970):19.

40. *Mountain*, p. 181. ". . .sa montagne en toute vérité," *Montagne*, p. 217.

41. *Mountain*, p. 185. "La montagne de son imagination n'avait presque rien de la montagne de l'Ungava. . . . Et sans doute ne s'agissait-il plus de savoir qui avait le mieux réussi sa montagne, Dieu ou Pierre, mais que lui aussi avait fait œuvre de créateur." *Montagne*, p. 221.

42. Roy, quoted in Cameron, *Conversations*, p. 144.

43. *Mountain,* p. 186. "Son âme resta un instant encore liée à l'œuvre parfaite enfin entrevue. Il fallait lui donner la vie, ne pas la laisser, elle, mourir. Ce qui meurt d'inexprimé, avec une vie, lui parut la seule mort regrettable." *Montagne,* p. 222.

Chapter Six

1. Phyllis Grosskurth, "Gentle Quebec," *Canadian Literature,* no. 49 (1971), p. 84.

2. S. Swan, "Windflower," *Toronto Telegram,* 19 September 1970, Section 3, p. 3.

3. Robert Dickson, "Un échec pour Gabrielle Roy?", *Le Soleil* (Québec), 31 October 1970, p. 37.

4. Pierre-Henri Simon, *"La Rivière sans repos,"* *Le Monde,* 25 February 1972, p. 13.

5. P. Sypnovich, "Another Gem of a Book," *Toronto Daily Star,* 22 September 1970, p. 36.

6. Nicole Lavigne, *"La Rivière sans repos,"* *L'Equipe,* January 1971, p. 19.

7. Paule Saint-Onge, "Retour de trois grands écrivains féminins," *Châtelaine* (Montréal), December 1970, p. 10.

8. Jean Ethier-Blais, "Gabrielle Roy," *Le Devoir* (Montréal), 28 November 1970, p. 12.

9. Ray Chatelin, "Another Book Top Writer," *Province* (Vancouver), 13 November 1970, p. 23.

10. *Windflower,* trans. Joyce Marshall. New Canadian Library (Toronto, 1970), p. 47. " 'Mais parce que c'est Jimmy.' . . . 'Eh oui! fit-il: il n'y aura qu'un Jimmy, comme il n'y a et il n'y aura jamais qu'une Elsa. Malgré notre multitude pareille à celle du sable, à l'infini, nous sommes tous, chacun de nous un être à part.' " *La Rivière sans repos,* Québec 10/10 (1970, reprint ed., Montréal, 1979), p. 177; hereafter this work cited as *Rivière.*

11. *Windflower,* p. 109. "Si elle jetait alors un coup d'œil devant elle sur l'avenir toujours aussi brumeux, il lui paraissait néanmoins devoir l'éloigner de plus en plus de sa vraie nature, l'entraîner loin d'elle-même. Elle ne voyait vraiment pas vers quoi elle allait. . . . Elle se voyait donc condamnée à avancer à travers l'inconnu." *Rivière,* p. 261.

12. *Windflower,* pp. 151–52. "Puis elle se penchait pour ramasser des riens: . . . ces filaments de plante, fins, blonds et soyeux comme des cheveux d'enfant, qui sont faits pour porter au loin des graines voyageuses. Elle les détachait brin à brin et soufflait dessus, son visage abîmé tout souriant de les voir monter et se répandre dans le soir." *Rivière,* p. 315.

13. P. Sypnovich, "Another Gem," p. 36.

14. *Enchanted Summer,* p. 56. "Le fleuve et la vie, tous deux en mouve-

ment, nous semblaient proches l'un et l'autre, encore que le fleuve dans son mouvement nous soit repos, alors que la vie souvent nous donne du mal à tâcher à la suivre." *Cet été qui chantait,* p. 93.

15. *Windflower,* pp. 37–38. "C'est, par excellence, le chemin mystérieux par lequel on est conduit à sa propre découverte. Tel qui commence dans un pauvre terre peut donner une fleur rare." *Rivière,* p. 164.

16. *Windflower,* p. 85. "Grâce à la guerre et au mélange du sang, se formera peut-être donc à la fin la race humaine. . . . une seule famille, toutes les nations réunies." *Rivière,* pp. 226–27.

17. See "Man and His World," in *Lights,* pp. 191–222. "Terre des Hommes," in *Lumières,* pp. 199–233.

Chapter Seven

1. Chadbourne, "Two Visions of the Prairie," in *The New Land,* p. 112.

2. Carol Shields, "The Loneliness of the Half-landed Immigrant," *Books in Canada,* November 1977, p. 35.

3. *Garden in the Wind,* trans. Alan Brown. (Toronto, 1977), p. 9. "Raconte ma vie," *Un jardin au bout du monde* (Montréal, 1975), p. 9; hereafter cited as *Garden* and *Jardin,* respectively.

4. Paul Socken, "Fellowship," *Canadian Forum,* February 1978, p. 36.

5. Gabrielle Poulin, *"Un jardin au bout du monde,"* in *Romans du pays* (Montréal: Bellarmin, 1980), p. 329.

6. *Garden,* p. 23. " 'Mais la Marcelline. . . parlait-elle de moi de temps en temps?' L'homme assura chaudement: 'Ah, pour sûr! Elle m'a souvent parlé de son frère. . .' 'Arthur,' précisa mon père. 'C'est bien ça: Arthur!' " *Jardin,* p. 25.

7. *Garden,* p. 41. " 'Je suis Barthélémy, dit-il, le garçon de votre frère Alcide. Je viens de Saint-Jérôme; c'est de Saint-Jérôme que je viens.' Puis il soupira: . . . 'Voyons! vous me reconnaissez pas; je suis Honoré, l'Honoré au père Phidime qu'on avait cru mort.' " *Jardin,* pp. 50–51.

8. Robert Tremblay, "L'Emouvant et beau retour de Gabrielle Roy," *Le Soleil* (Québec), 28 June 1975, p. 17.

9. *Garden,* p. 150. "Pourquoi inventer une autre histoire, et serait-elle plus proche de la réalité que ne le sont en eux-mêmes les faits? . . . Ce fut un rêve, pas autre chose!" *Jardin,* pp. 155–56.

10. *Garden,* p. 9. "Il n'y avait peut-être que moi à avoir imaginé son existence et par conséquent à pouvoir lui donner vie." *Jardin,* p. 8.

11. *Garden,* p. 67. "Un immense manège où personne ne comprenait jamais personne." *Jardin,* p. 82.

12. Dudek, *First Person in Literature,* pp. 15–16.

13. Yves Thériault, "Les Enfants de la vie de Gabrielle Roy," *L'Express* (Montréal), 7 April 1978, p. 8.

14. Gilles Marcotte, "Gabrielle Roy et l'institutrice passionnée," *Le Devoir* (Montréal), 24 September 1977, p. 15.

15. Thuong Vuong Riddick, "Gabrielle Roy dans la plénitude de son art," *Le Devoir* (Montréal), 20 October 1977, p. 20.

16. Gabrielle Poulin, "Une merveilleuse histoire d'amour" in *Romans du pays,* p. 356.

17. William French, "Vignettes," *Globe and Mail* (Toronto), 24 February 1979, p. 38.

18. Jacques Godbout, "Gabrielle Roy," *Le Magazine Maclean,* September 1975, p. 77.

19. *Children of My Heart,* trans. Alan Brown (Toronto, 1979) p. 117. ". . . ce passioné besoin . . . de lutter pour obtenir le meilleur en chacun." *Ces enfants de ma vie* (Montréal, 1977), p. 139; hereafter cited as *Children* and *Enfants,* respectively.

20. *Children,* p. 125. "Je voyais passer sur son visage le frémissement joyeux que lui avait procuré la sensation de tenir, tout consentant entre ses mains, le poisson le plus méfiant du monde, et me disais que ce serait bientôt son tour d'être pris, vulnérable comme je le découvrais, si moi-même je me montrais assez hostile." *Enfants,* p. 149.

21. *Children,* p. 164. "J'avais le sentiment de voir un enfant mourant sous la poussée impitoyable de l'homme qui va en naître." *Enfants,* p. 201.

Chapter Eight

1. Monique Genuist, *La Création romanesque chez Gabrielle Roy* (Montréal, 1966), p. 11.

2. M.-L. Gaulin, "Le Monde romanesque de Roger Lemelin et de Gabrielle Roy" in *Le Roman canadien-français,* Archives des lettres canadiennes, vol. 3 (Montréal: Fides, 1964), p. 143.

3. See Claude Jasmin, *Ethel et le Terroriste* (Montréal: Ed. de l'Homme, 1965).

4. See Hugh MacLennan, *Return of the Sphinx* (New York: Scribner, 1967).

5. Cameron, *Conversations,* p. 136.

6. Jacques Dufrèsne, quoted in Cobb, "Seasons," p. 14.

7. Alice Parizeau, "Gabrielle Roy, la grande romancière canadienne," *Châtelaine* (Montréal), April 1966, p. 120.

8. Emilia B. Allaire, "Notre grande romancière: Gabrielle Roy," *L'Action catholique* (Montréal), 5 June 1960, p. 16.

9. Cameron, *Conversations,* p. 130.

10. Ibid., p. 133.

11. Ibid., p. 134.

Selected Bibliography

PRIMARY SOURCES

Listed below are the French and English editions from which we have quoted in this volume. The original date of publication appears in parentheses.

1. Adult Fiction

Alexandre Chenevert. Montréal: Stanké, (1954) 1979, Collection: Québec 10/10. Translated by Harry Binsse as *The Cashier.* Toronto: McClelland & Stewart, (1955) 1970, New Canadian Library. Introduction by W. C. Lougheed.

Bonheur d'occasion. Montréal: Stanké, (1945) 1978, Collection: Québec 10/10. Translated by Hannah Josephson as *The Tin Flute.* Toronto: McClelland & Stewart, (1947) 1958, New Canadian Library. Introduction by Hugo McPherson.

Ces enfants de ma vie. Montréal: Stanké, 1977. Translated by Alan Brown as *Children of My Heart.* Toronto: McClelland & Stewart, 1979.

Cet été qui chantait. Montréal: Stanké, (1972) 1979, Collection: Québec 10/10. Translated by Joyce Marshall as *Enchanted Summer.* Toronto: McClelland & Stewart, 1976.

De quoi t'ennuies-tu, Eveline? Montreal: Editions du Sentier, 1982.

Un jardin au bout du monde. Montréal: Beauchemin, 1975. Translated by Alan Brown as *Garden in the Wind.* Toronto: McClelland & Stewart, 1977.

La Montagne secrète. Montréal: Stanké, (1961) 1978, Collection: Québec 10/10. Translated by Harry Binsse as *The Hidden Mountain.* Toronto: McClelland & Stewart, (1962) 1975, New Canadian Library. Introduction by Malcolm Ross.

La Petite Poule d'Eau. Montréal: Stanké, (1950) 1980, Collection: Québec 10/10. Translated by Harry Binsse as *Where Nests the Water Hen.* Toronto: McClelland & Stewart, (1951) 1970, New Canadian Library. Introduction by Gordon Roper.

La Rivière sans repos, roman, précédé de Trois nouvelles esquimaudes. Montréal: Stanké, (1970) 1979, Collection: Québec 10/10. Translated by Joyce Marshall as *Windflower* (novel only). Toronto: McClelland &

Stewart, (1970), 1975, New Canadian Library. Introduction by Lorraine McMullen.

La Route d'Altamont. Montréal: Editions HMH, 1966, Collection: L'Arbre. Translated by Joyce Marshall as *The Road Past Altamont*. Toronto: McClelland & Stewart, 1966.

Rue Deschambault. Montréal: Stanké, (1955) 1980, Collection: Québec 10/10. Translated by Harry Binsse as *Street of Riches*. Toronto: McClelland & Stewart, (1957) 1967, New Canadian Library. Introduction by Brandon Conron.

2. Miscellaneous Writings

"L'Arbre" (essai) in *Cahiers de l'Académie canadienne-française* 13. Montréal: Académie canadienne-française, 1970, pp. 5–27.

Fragiles lumières de la terre, écrits divers 1942–1970. Montréal: Quinze, 1978. Translated by Alan Brown as *The Fragile Lights of Earth*. Toronto: McClelland & Stewart, 1982.

"Jeux du romancier et des lecteurs." In Marc Gagné, *Visages de Gabrielle Roy*. Montréal: Beauchemin, 1973, pp. 263–72.

"Préface." In *René Richard*. Québec: Musée du Québec, 1967, pp. 3–6.

"Témoignage." In *Le Roman canadien-français*. Archives des lettres canadiennes. Montréal: Fides, 1964, pp. 302–6.

3. Children's Books

Courte-Queue. Montréal: Stanké, 1979. Translated by Alan Brown as *Cliptail*. Toronto: McClelland & Stewart, 1980. Illustrations by François Olivier (English and French editions).

Ma Vache Bossie. Montréal: Leméac, 1976. Illustrations de Louise Pomminville.

SECONDARY SOURCES

1. Bibliographies

Gagné, Marc. "Bibliographie." In *Visages de Gabrielle Roy*. Montréal: Beauchemin, 1973, pp. 287–320. Very useful reference. Comprehensive listings for works to *La Rivière sans repos*.

Socken, Paul. "Gabrielle Roy, an Annotated Bibliography." Vol. 1, edited by Robert Lecker and Jack David. Downsview: ECW Press, 1979, pp. 213–63. An excellent source of reference.

2. Books and Parts of Books

Bessette, Gérard. "Correspondence entre les personnages et le milieu physique dans *Bonheur d'occasion*" and "Interview avec Gabrielle Roy." In

Une littérature en ébullition. Montréal: Jour, 1968, pp. 257–77, 303–8. Stimulating article by a critic and novelist. Roy is reluctant to respond to Bessette's interpretations of her works.

————. *"Alexandre Chenevert* de Gabrielle Roy" and *"La Route d'Altamont* clef de *La Montagne secrète* de Gabrielle Roy." In *Trois romanciers québecois*. Montréal: Jour, 1973, pp. 185–99, 203–37. Thought-provoking study on motivation and psychological interpretations.

Brochu, André. "Thèmes et structures dans *Bonheur d'occasion*." In *L'Instance critique*, 1961–1973. Montréal: Leméac, 1974, pp. 204–46. Significant study. Brochu suggests a fundamental opposition exists between Roy's feminine world and her masculine world, symbolized by the circle and straight line, respectively.

Cameron, Donald. "Gabrielle Roy: A Bird in the Prison Window." In *Conversations with Canadian Novelists*. Toronto: Macmillan, 1973, pp. 128–45. Excellent. Gabrielle Roy discusses her works in a most informative manner.

Gagné, Marc. *Visages de Gabrielle Roy*. Montréal: Beauchemin, 1973. Sympathetic and stimulating study. Highlights Roy's optimism and concept of progress.

Genuist, Monique. *La Création romanesque chez Gabrielle Roy*. Montréal: Le Cercle du Livre de France, 1966. A very effective introduction for Roy's early works.

Grandpré, Pierre de. "Le Lait de la tendresse humaine." In *Dix ans de vie littéraire au Canada français*. Montréal: Beauchemin, 1966, pp. 91–94. Sympathetic analysis of *Rue Deschambault*. Interesting comparisons with French and English-speaking authors.

Grosskurth, Phyllis. *Gabrielle Roy*. Canadian Writers and Their Works. Toronto: Forum House, 1972. This monograph includes excellent, detailed plot summaries of Roy's works to *The Road Past Altamont*.

Hind-Smith, Joan. "The Life of Gabrielle Roy." In *Three Voices*. Toronto: Clarke, Irwin, 1975, pp. 62–126. Interesting biographical details.

Ricard, François. *Gabrielle Roy*. Ecrivains canadiens d'aujourd'hui. Montréal: Fides, 1975. Best available study. Most sympathetic. Highlights the dichotomies or "insoluble paradoxes" in Roy's works and her attempt to re-create the world of her childhood.

Robidoux, Réjean and André Renaud. *"Bonheur d'occasion."* In *Le Roman canadien-français du vingtième siècle*. Ottawa: Editions de l'Université d'Ottawa, 1966, pp. 75–91. Stresses that the complexity of *Bonheur d'occasion* is unprecedented in French-Canadian literature. Important stylistic analysis.

Saint-Pierre, Annette. *Gabrielle Roy sous le signe du rêve*. Saint-Boniface: Editions du Blé, 1975. Interesting material. Strong emphasis on psychological theories.

Shek, Ben-Zion. *"Bonheur d'occasion"* and *"Alexandre Chenevert."* In *Social Realism in the French-Canadian Novel*. Montreal: Harvest House, 1977, pp. 65–111, 173–203. Approach to French-Canadian literature in terms of social, political, and economic considerations provides important, new insights.

3. Articles

Blais, Jacques. "L'Unité organique de *Bonheur d'occasion.*" *Etudes françaises* 6 (1970): 25–50. Excellent structural analysis. Responds to André Brochu's pessimism regarding irreconcilable opposites by focusing on Emmanuel and the novel's conclusion.

Brown, Alan. "Gabrielle Roy and the Temporary Provincial." *Tamarack Review* 1 (1956): 61–70. Interesting. Interprets works in terms of a "dialogue of innocence and experience."

Hayne, David M. "Gabrielle Roy." *Canadian Modern Language Review* 21 (1964): 20–26. Excellent introductory study of early works.

LeGrand, Albert. "Gabrielle Roy ou l'être partagé." *Etudes françaises* 1 (1965): 39–65. Interesting article with the emphasis on opposing values.

McPherson, Hugo. "The Garden and the Cage: The Achievement of Gabrielle Roy." *Canadian Literature* 1 (1959): 46–57. Interesting response to Alan Brown's article. Concludes that Alexandre Chenevert provides the key to our urban existence.

Marcotte, Gilles. "En relisant *Bonheur d'occasion.*" *L'Action nationale* 35 (1950): 197–206. Emphasizes universal aspects and suggests comparisons between Roy and Péguy.

Murphy, John J. "Visit with Gabrielle Roy." *Thought, Fordham University Quarterly* 38 (1963): 447–55. Good. Interesting discussion about Alexandre Chenevert and death.

Parizeau, Alice. "Gabrielle Roy, la grande romancière canadienne." *Châtelaine* (Montréal), April 1966, pp. 44, 118, 120–22, 137, 140. Sympathetic. Interview emphasizes Roy's role as an artist and the role of women in contemporary society.

Ricard, François. "Gabrielle Roy, 30 ans d'écriture: le cercle enfin uni des hommes." *Liberté* 18, no. 103 (1976): 59–78. Excellent. Focuses on the tension between the ideal and the real in Roy's work.

Socken, Paul. " 'Le Pays de l'amour' in the Works of Gabrielle Roy." *Revue de l'Université d'Ottawa* 46 (1976): 309–23. Interesting discussion on utopianism in Roy's work.

Thério, Adrien. "Le Portrait du père dans *Rue Deschambault* de Gabrielle Roy." *Livres et auteurs québécois 1969.* Quebec: Les Presses de l'Université Laval, 1970, pp. 237–43. Sympathetic response to criticism that Roy's male characters are less complex than her women.

Index

96455

HESSE, MARTA

DATE DUE
